FREE VIDEO  **FREE VIDEO**

Essential Test Tips Video from Trivium Test Prep!

Dear Customer,

Thank you for purchasing from Trivium Test Prep! We're honored to help you prepare for your exam.

To show our appreciation, we're offering a **FREE** *Essential Test Tips* **Video by Trivium Test Prep**.* Our video includes 35 test preparation strategies that will make you successful on your exam. All we ask is that you email us your feedback and describe your experience with our product. Amazing, awful, or just so-so: we want to hear what you have to say!

To receive your **FREE** *Essential Test Tips* **Video,** please email us at 5star@triviumtestprep.com. Include "Free 5 Star" in the subject line and the following information in your email:

1. The title of the product you purchased.
2. Your rating from 1 – 5 (with 5 being the best).
3. Your feedback about the product, including how our materials helped you meet your goals and ways in which we can improve our products.
4. Your full name and shipping address so we can send your **FREE** *Essential Test Tips* **Video**.

If you have any questions or concerns please feel free to contact us directly at: 5star@ triviumtestprep.com.

Thank you!

– Trivium Test Prep Team

*To get access to the free video please email us at 5star@triviumtestprep.com, and please follow the instructions above.

LSAT Study Guide 2022-2023:

STUDY GUIDE WITH REAL PRACTICE EXAMS
AND ANSWER EXPLANATIONS
FOR ALL CONCEPTS ON
THE LAW SCHOOL ADMISSION TEST

ELISSA SIMON

Table of Contents

Introduction

Congratulations on your decision to study law—few other professions are so rewarding! By purchasing this book, you've already taken the first step toward succeeding in your career. The next step is to do well on the LSAT (Law School Admission Test), which will require you to demonstrate ability in analytical reasoning, logical reasoning, and reading comprehension.

This book will walk you through the important concepts in each of these subjects and provide you with inside information on test strategies and tactics. Even if it's been years since you graduated from high school or cracked open a textbook, don't worry—this book contains everything you'll need for the LSAT.

What Is the LSAT?

The Law School Admission Test (LSAT) is administered by the Law School Admission Council (LSAC) to candidates for law school admission. Law schools in the United States, Canada, and countries around the world use the LSAT as part of their admissions process to gauge the skills and potential of applicants.

Specifically, the LSAT tests reading comprehension, analytical reasoning, and logical reasoning. There is a writing section, which may be completed separately.

The LSAT is offered throughout the year. Candidates may take the LSAT up to three times in any rolling two-year period.

What Is a "Disclosed" LSAT?

The LSAT is administered several times throughout the year. Only three tests per year are disclosed. A **disclosed** test is released to test takers after it is administered. Disclosed tests allow examinees to see exactly which questions they answered correctly and incorrectly, reviewing their scores in depth.

Test takers who take a disclosed LSAT will receive, in addition to their scores, their score band, percentile rank, a copy of the answer sheet, and a copy of the scored sections to analyze their results.

For nondisclosed tests, examinees will only receive their score and percentile rank. They will not receive a copy of the test, nor will they receive a list of which questions were answered incorrectly.

Disclosed tests are never readministered.

What's on the LSAT?

The LSAT tests three topics: logical reasoning, analytical reasoning, and reading comprehension. All questions are multiple choice, with five answer choices.

Candidates may also choose to sit for the Writing Sample the same day or eight days prior (see below). LSAT scores will not be released until the Writing Sample is completed.

There are four required sections: one logical reasoning section, one analytical reasoning section, one reading comprehension section, and an experimental, unscored section. The unscored section allows LSAC to test new questions for future use. However, you will not know which section is unscored, so be sure to answer all the questions.

For examinees who take the optional writing sample on the same day, the test takes about three hours, not including breaks. Examinees receive a short, ten-minute break after the second section.

WHAT'S on the LSAT?		
SECTION	**QUESTIONS**	**TIME**
Reading Comprehension	26 – 28	35 minutes
Logical Reasoning 1	24 – 26	35 minutes
Analytical Reasoning	23 – 24	35 minutes
Experimental Section (unscored)	24 – 26	35 minutes
Writing Sample (optional, but must complete within the year)	1 prompt	35 minutes
Total	**Approx. 104 questions + writing sample**	**Approx. 3 hours**

The Writing Sample

The Writing Sample can be completed up to eight days before the LSAT. See https://www.lsac.org/lsat/taking-lsat/about-lsat-writing for details.

Scoring

The number of questions answered correctly comprises the raw score. That number is then converted to a scaled score ranging from 120 to 180. The highest possible score is 180. Test takers who take a disclosed test will receive a score report and be able to determine which questions were answered incorrectly.

How Is the LSAT Administered?

The LSAT is administered digitally. There are no paper answer sheets; test takers tap their answer choice on the screen.

Registration for the LSAT is handled by the LSAC. Go to http://www.lsac.org for the most current details and to register.

Taking the LSAT (including the Writing Sample) costs $200. However, additional fees are required to send your scores to law schools. Check https://www.lsac.org/lsat/lsat-dates-deadlines-score-release-dates/lsat-cas-fees for details and additional pricing packages.

You will need to sign up for LSAC's **Credential Assembly Service** to submit your transcripts and letters of recommendation. This includes an additional fee.

On test day, you may not bring your cell phone or any electronic device into the building where you are taking the LSAT. Unlike other testing centers, lockers may not be provided for personal effects, so leave your cell phone at home or in your car. Check with your testing center ahead of time for details.

You must bring a current, valid ID that contains both your name (exactly matching your LSAC account) and a photo. Check https://www.lsac.org/lsat-test-center-regulations for current details on required identification and test day policy.

HELPFUL HINT

Test Tip: LSAC also makes a full practice test available.

How to Use This Book

As you work through this book, these should be among your goals:

1. **Learn how the test works**: Make sure you know what to expect on test day. You won't know what they're going to ask you, but you should be well prepared for *how* they're going to ask it. Learn how the test works, what kind of questions you'll be asked, and how to use reason to find the answers to the questions.

2. **Read and work through different types of questions**: Do a few practice questions for each question type. This will give you a feel for the difficulty and structure of LSAT questions.

3. **Master the logical concepts in the Fundamentals section**: This book is concise, but this means that a lot of information is packed into a few sentences. Reread these sections until you are so comfortable with the concepts that you could teach them to someone else.

4. **Take a practice test**: Once you have learned some of the fundamentals, take a practice test or a thirty-five-minute section of a test. If you find the time limit difficult, then you should take more untimed practice tests until you've learned the material.

5. **Diagnose and review**: As you work through practice problems, spend time reviewing your work. This reinforces what you are doing correctly and clarifies errors.

6. **Target your weaknesses and improve**: As you review your completed tests, take note of the types of questions you're missing, and use this book to hone your skills in those areas. Draft sample LSAT questions. Explain the concepts to a friend. Create arguments out of real-life scenarios, and ask every LSAT question you can think of about each of these arguments: Is it sound? How would you strengthen it? Weaken it? Justify it? Identify the types of questions you're missing, and then work through the respective sections in this book.

Preparing for the LSAT: Materials

Copies of actual, officially administered LSAT tests are available for the public to purchase. Candidates may wish to complete several full practice tests under timed conditions before taking the official LSAT.

Preparation Materials from 2007 and Earlier

The tests from 2007 to present, for example, include the new Comparative Reading passage in the Reading Comprehension section; older tests do not. Additionally, tests from 2012 to present provide two pages of space to work on each Logic Game, whereas the older tests present each game on one page.

The LSAT has undergone a few other minor changes:

- Recent Logical Reasoning sections have included more Sufficient Assumption questions than in the past.

- Recent Reading Comprehension passages are often viewed as more difficult.

- Some Logic Games from the early 1990s included a predesigned diagram as part of the rules.

- Recent tests tend to have less ambiguous wording.

- The thirty-five-minute, unscored writing sample may be taken separately from the rest of the exam.

Test-Taking Tips

Trust Yourself

The LSAT is simply a test of your ability to think logically and methodically. There is no one best way to solve the questions on the LSAT.

On the LSAT, you'll have to put aside your own notions of right and wrong and focus on evaluating whether the arguments presented are logically sound. Whether they are factually true in real life is irrelevant.

An answer is never wrong because "it's too easy." If your confidence is faltering on test day, resolve to go with your gut instinct instead of second-guessing yourself.

Focus on the Big Picture

It is easy to get lost in the details, both on the LSAT and in law school. LSAT questions will reference unfamiliar people, situations, or terms. These details are not important; solving the question is what matters.

- In Logical Reasoning, just worry about the big picture: Separate the facts from the conclusion(s) in each argument and focus on answering the question at hand.
- In Analytical Reasoning, focus on wrapping your mind around the rules of each game.
- In Reading Comprehension, develop a grasp of what the author is trying to prove to the reader.

Manage Your Time

Logical Reasoning: You will have an average of one minute and twenty-four seconds (1:24) per question. Pace yourself. On a Logical Reasoning section, the most difficult questions tend to fall between questions 11 and 21. Aim to complete the first ten questions in ten minutes; that way, you'll have ample time for the remaining questions. Remember that all questions have equal worth, so skip (or guess on) a question that poses a risk of consuming too much time.

Logic Games: Allow three minutes to set up each of the four games, and one minute to answer each of the (approximately) twenty-three questions.

Reading Comprehension: Allot approximately eight minutes and forty-five seconds per passage. This includes reading the passage and answering the questions.

1 Fundamental Logical Concepts

This section is a general review of how arguments work and the various patterns of reasoning on the LSAT. While these fundamentals primarily apply to the Logical Reasoning sections of the LSAT, they are also relevant to the Analytical Reasoning (Logic Games) and Reading Comprehension sections.

Be sure to distinguish these types of arguments and argumentative techniques from the actual questions you will be asked on the LSAT.

These patterns of reasoning densely populate the LSAT Logical Reasoning sections. For any given argument, you may be asked many possible questions. Understanding the pattern of reasoning in each argument will help you determine what might be missing from an argument.

These patterns of reasoning also appear in the Reading Comprehension section. Many authors incorporate analogies or examples, often either advocating a suggestion or predicting an outcome.

Finally, the conditional statements, either-or patterns, and principle application subjects are relevant to the Logic Games, where you will be given a set of rules to apply to various scenarios. Be careful not to confuse necessary and sufficient conditions.

How Arguments Work

Premises, Conclusions, and Assumptions in Arguments

How do arguments work? Let's begin by examining a simple argument:

> **Premise**: Laura drives a blue Ford Focus.
>
> **Premise**: Laura gets twenty-five miles per gallon.
>
> **Conclusion**: Therefore, if Jordan buys a blue Ford Focus, Jordan will also get at least twenty-five miles per gallon.

This is an argument. The components of an argument are premises and conclusions. You make arguments all the time in your daily life: based on facts (premises), you give the opinion (conclusion) that you want someone else to believe.

In any argument, there is at least one premise and at least one conclusion. Your **conclusion** is whatever you are trying to prove. **Premises** are the facts, evidence, or other supports you provide to back up your conclusion.

Certain words and phrases signal a conclusion: *therefore, so, thus, accordingly, consequently, as a result, hence.*

Other words signal a premise: *because, since, for, seeing as, in light of the fact that.*

Note that the conclusion is not necessarily the last sentence of an argument. For example, the preceding argument would be logically identical if it said, "Jordan will get at least twenty-five miles per gallon if he buys a blue Ford Focus, because Laura drives a blue Ford Focus, and Laura gets twenty-five miles per gallon."

The order of sentences within an argument does not matter on the LSAT. That said, it may help to first read the premises, and then say to yourself, "Therefore," followed by the conclusion. Untangle arguments in this way as you encounter them. Isolate the conclusion from the facts, and see whether the facts provided support the conclusion offered.

Argument Versus Explanation

Note the difference between these two passages:

> **1.** The meteor that landed in Mexico 63 million years ago killed the dinosaurs. It caused earthquakes and tidal waves, and it kicked up clouds of dust that gave the dinosaurs fatal respiratory diseases.
>
> **2.** The meteor that landed in Mexico 63 million years ago must have killed the dinosaurs, because it caused earthquakes, tidal waves, and lingering dust clouds just before the dinosaurs went extinct, and there are no other known events that could have killed all of the dinosaurs.

The first passage is mere **explanation**. There is no argument here because the passage simply presents two facts. It does not tell us that one of the statements is true because the other statement is true.

The second passage is an **argument**. The first clause ("The meteor... must have killed the dinosaurs") is the conclusion. The word *because* indicates that what follows are the premises. This is an argument because the passage tells us that the first clause follows logically from the second.

In Logical Reasoning sections, most passages are arguments. However, there are some question types that are occasionally accompanied by bare fact sets, not by arguments. Specifically, the passages that accompany Inference questions and Resolve the Paradox questions may sometimes be fact sets rather than actual arguments.

 **HELPFUL HINT**
Note that there does not need to be an actual debate or disagreement in order to have an argument. *Argument* does not mean "debate" in the logical sense; rather, it is a set of one or more premises offered in support of one or more conclusions.

For all question types, take care to distinguish the author's premises from the conclusions.

Strong and Weak Arguments

An argument is **strong** if the conclusion is very likely to follow from the premises. An argument is **weak** if there is great uncertainty as to whether the conclusion will follow from the premises. Keep in mind that strength has nothing to do with truth.

For example, this argument is very strong:

> Almost everyone who wears blue tends to score above 170 on the LSAT. Almost everyone who scores above 170 on the LSAT wears blue. Therefore, a large group of LSAT takers who wear green is likely to have a lower average LSAT score than a large group of LSAT takers who wear blue.

This argument may be ridiculous, but so are many of the arguments you will encounter on the LSAT. Based on the premises (everything before "therefore"), the conclusion follows logically.

Let's review the Ford Focus argument, which is moderately strong. Consider these facts: Laura drives a blue Ford Focus, and she gets twenty-five miles per gallon. That does not guarantee that Jordan will also get the same gas mileage if he buys a blue Ford Focus.

For example, we do not know anything about Laura and Jordan's driving habits; maybe Laura drives entirely on rural highways, whereas Jordan drives in urban traffic. If this were true, then our conclusion (that Jordan will get twenty-five miles per gallon) would be less likely, because Jordan's driving habits are less fuel efficient.

Consider the following premises that would weaken this argument (we call these "weakeners"):

- Laura's car is new, but Jordan's car is older and less fuel efficient.
- Jordan tows more weight than Laura.
- Jordan uses more air-conditioning than Laura.
- Laura optimizes her fuel efficiency with regular maintenance, whereas Jordan does not.

As you add each of these additional premises to your original argument, the argument becomes weaker and weaker:

> **Premises**: Laura drives a blue Ford Focus and gets twenty-five miles per gallon. Jordan also buys a blue Ford Focus, but he buys an older one, tows more weight, drives more in the city, uses more air-conditioning, and foregoes regular maintenance.
>
> **Conclusion**: But Jordan will still get at least twenty-five miles per gallon.

This is an example of a weak argument, with all that additional evidence indicating a poorly supported conclusion.

Now, what if we wanted to make the argument stronger? There are three ways to do this (strengtheners):

1. Add in a new premise that rules out a potential weakener.

2. Add in a new premise that makes the conclusion more likely. (This may overlap with number 1, but it goes beyond merely ruling out the potential weakener.)

3. Add in a new premise that makes the conclusion 100 percent certain.

Table 1.1 contains examples of these strengtheners.

TABLE 1.1. Weakeners and Strengtheners	
WEAKENERS	• Laura's car is new, but Jordan's car is older and less fuel efficient. • Jordan tows more weight than Laura. • Jordan uses more air-conditioning than Laura. • Laura optimizes her fuel efficiency with regular maintenance, whereas Jordan does not.
STRENGTHENERS	• Jordan's car is at least as new as Laura's. • Jordan does not tow more weight than Laura. • Jordan does not use more air-conditioning than Laura. • Jordan performs the same fuel-efficiency-optimizing maintenance Laura performs. *These strengtheners operate by ruling out potential weakeners.* • Jordan's Focus has a smaller, more fuel-efficient engine than Laura's. • Jordan drives entirely on country roads, where he maximizes his fuel efficiency. *These operate by making the conclusion more likely.* • The only factor that affects fuel efficiency is the model of the car. • All cars of the same color get the same mileage per gallon. *These not only strengthen the argument, but also fully justify it.*

Let's detail those three different ways of strengthening the argument:

1. Ruling Out Potential Weakeners

    All of the strengtheners in the first set *negate* premises that would weaken the argument. These strengtheners are also necessary assumptions; that is, in making the argument that Jordan will get twenty-five miles per gallon, the author *must necessarily assume* that Jordan's car will be at least as new as Laura's and that Jordan will not tow more weight, use more air-conditioning, or perform poorer maintenance than Laura. If the author did not assume these things, there would be no way for the author to conclude that Jordan will get the same gas mileage as Laura. These statements are called **assumptions** because the author has not actually stated them in the argument, so they are unstated premises. If we add these sentences to the argument as **stated premises** that we know are true, then the conclusion would become more likely.

2. Adding Anything That Makes the Conclusion More Likely

The strengtheners in the second group go beyond merely negating potential weakeners. The first statement does not merely say that Jordan's car is as fuel efficient as Laura's, but rather that it is *more* fuel efficient than Laura's. This absolutely does rule out a potential weakener (it rules out "Laura's car is more fuel efficient than Jordan's"), but it goes further. By telling us that Jordan's car is *more* fuel efficient, the likelihood that Jordan will receive twenty-five or more miles per gallon is even higher.

3. Adding a Premise to Prove the Conclusion with 100 Percent Certainty

The strengtheners in the third group qualify not only as strengtheners, but as sufficient assumptions. Sufficient assumptions are statements that would turn our otherwise mediocre argument into a certain one. Adding either one of the premises listed would make our conclusion 100 percent inescapable.

Take the first one, for example:

> **Premise (added):** The only factor that affects fuel efficiency is the model of the car.
>
> **Premise (original):** Laura drives a blue Ford Focus.
>
> **Premise (original):** Laura gets twenty-five miles per gallon.
>
> **Conclusion:** Therefore, if Jordan buys a blue Ford Focus, Jordan will also get at least twenty-five miles per gallon.

Now that we have added in a strengthener, there is no way out of the conclusion; Jordan is buying the same model car as Laura, so Jordan will get the same fuel efficiency as Laura.

These kinds of strengtheners are called sufficient assumptions because if you assume the statement to be true, it is enough to make the conclusion certain. They are discussed in detail in the next section.

If we were worried about analyzing the factual correctness of our argument, we would be correct to object to the statement "The only factor that affects fuel efficiency is the model of the car." Factually speaking, this statement is false in real life.

However, logical validity is a separate inquiry from factual correctness. The LSAT tests your ability to use logic and reason. Thus, you might need to add in an unlikely premise (like "All cars of the same color get the same mileage per gallon") to make an argument stronger. Consider the following argument, which is absurd but logically valid:

> **Premise**: All spiders have wings.
>
> **Premise**: Anything with wings can fly.
>
> **Conclusion**: Therefore, all spiders can fly.

Necessary and Sufficient Assumptions

The following is a common point of confusion among even the most adept LSAT candidates, so read carefully.

Necessary assumptions are unstated premises that the author must believe to make an argument. If the author were not assuming these premises, she would not be able to make the argument and believe that the conclusion was plausible.

When LSAT questions ask you to identify a necessary assumption, they are asking you to identify something that must be true based on the information stated in the argument—something that the conclusion requires in order to stand.

If a necessary assumption were false, it would destroy the argument. Similarly, if you negate a necessary assumption, you end up with a factor that severely weakens or destroys the argument.

On the other hand, the author does not necessarily believe sufficient assumptions. **Sufficient assumptions** are statements that would fully justify the argument and render its conclusion valid, if the reader assumed them to be true.

In Logical Reasoning questions, you will be asked to justify conclusions. That requires making an argument perfectly strong by adding in a sufficient assumption. In Analytical Reasoning (Logic Games), you must figure out what information would be sufficient to determine all of the variables in the game—again, by adding in an assumption that is sufficient to draw conclusions about the remaining variables.

Usually, you can craft a statement that is both necessary and sufficient for an argument to work. Take this argument, for example:

> **Premise**: You're bleeding!
>
> **Conclusion**: So, you must need a bandage.

This is an ordinary argument that someone might make. The argument they are actually making is:

> **Premise**: You're bleeding!
>
> **Unstated premise (assumption)**: People who are bleeding need bandages.
>
> **Conclusion**: So, you must need a bandage.

Of course, you would never say to someone, "Oh, you're bleeding! And people who are bleeding need bandages. So, you must need a bandage." Nevertheless, you have an unstated premise that people who are bleeding need bandages. If you did not believe that, then you would not be able to argue your conclusion. Furthermore, because our stated premise is "You're bleeding," adding in this unstated premise is sufficient to prove our conclusion ("You must need a bandage").

Consider this argument:

> Property taxes are evil because they infringe on citizens' natural rights.
>
> **Premise**: Property taxes infringe on citizens' natural rights.
>
> **Conclusion**: Therefore, property taxes are evil.

An assumption that is both necessary and sufficient would be: Things that infringe on citizens' natural rights are evil.

An assumption that is necessary but not sufficient to prove the conclusion would be: Not all things that infringe on citizens' rights are good.

An assumption that is sufficient but not necessary to prove the conclusion would be: Anything that infringes on anyone's rights is evil.

Table 1.2 summarizes necessary and sufficient assumptions.

HELPFUL HINT

Create your own arguments and practice identifying assumptions that are necessary, sufficient, and both necessary and sufficient. This will help your Logical Reasoning and Reading Comprehension skills.

TABLE 1.2. Necessary and Sufficient Assumptions

NECESSARY ASSUMPTIONS	SUFFICIENT ASSUMPTIONS
If the argument's conclusion is true, then the assumption must be true.	If the assumption is true, then the argument's conclusion must be true.
The *author* is making the assumption.	The *reader* is making the assumption to prove that the author is correct.
The assumption must be true (it is required; hence "necessary" assumption).	The assumption might be totally implausible. However, if the assumption were true, it would make the argument airtight.
If you add in this assumption, there might still be holes in the argument.	If you add in this assumption, there will be absolutely no holes in the argument.
If you negate this assumption, the argument will be severely weakened or fall apart entirely.	You can negate this assumption, and the argument may still follow logically.

LSAT Logic Vocabulary

There are no magic LSAT words. Every word on the LSAT is used according to a normal dictionary definition. However, if you have not had experience in analyzing arguments in the past, you might not know at first glance the differences between an analogy, an example, and an illustration. The terms and phrases on the following pages appear frequently in both Reading Comprehension and Logical Reasoning questions, so be sure you are familiar with them and can tell them apart.

Verbs

These verbs frequently appear in Logical Reasoning (on Method of Reasoning questions) and in Reading Comprehension (on Author's Purpose questions):

- state, set out, set forth, say, present
- overlook, ignore, fail to consider
- compare
- illustrate, demonstrate, exemplify
- show, prove, demonstrate
- dismiss, discredit, discount, disregard (to exclude or eliminate a proposition)
- cause, influence, foster, promote, induce, encourage, facilitate, lead to, produce
- assume, presuppose, take for granted
- appeal to, use, rely on
- justify, establish, allow the conclusion to be properly drawn
- strengthen, support, bolster, further, advance
- refute, disprove, deny, negate
- weaken, undermine, call into question, make vulnerable to criticism, cast doubt on

 DID YOU KNOW?

Imply vs. infer: To **imply** is to present propositions which, if true, result in some other proposition being true. To **infer** is to draw a conclusion from given premises. Statements imply. Readers infer.

Nouns

- **alternatives**: different options or ways of achieving a result
- **analogy**: an argument that uses the underlying reasoning in a similar situation and applies that reasoning to the situation in the primary argument
- **application**: a statement that draws a conclusion about an actual, specific case on the basis of a general principle
- **assumption**: an unstated premise
- **cause**: a factor whose occurrence results in the occurrence of some effect
- **claim** (conclusion): what the author is trying to prove as a logical consequence of the premises
- **conclusion** (claim): what the author is trying to prove as a logical consequence of the premises
- **condition**: a circumstance that affects the occurrence of another event (necessary conditions are required for the other event to occur; sufficient conditions ensure that the other event will occur)
- **consequence**: a result
- **contrapositive**: a conditional statement of the form ~B →~A, logically equivalent to A → B
- **correlation**: a relationship between two variables where the frequency of one variable is tied to the frequency of the other variable (either directly or inversely)

- **counterexample**: an illustration presented to refute a proposition
- **effect**: a phenomenon whose occurrence is the result of some other factor
- **event** (phenomenon): any observable behavior or occurrence
- **example**: an illustration of a proposition
- **fact** (support/premise/reason): evidence offered to prove a conclusion
- **general principle**: a broad statement that could apply to many cases and from which is drawn a conclusion about a specific case
- **historical fact**: any historical evidence from the past that is offered to prove a conclusion
- **hypothesis**: a theoretical belief that has not yet been proven true
- **illustration**: a statement that applies a general principle to a specific, actual situation
- **main idea/main point**: the conclusion (if an argument has only one conclusion) or the ultimate conclusion that is supported by all other conclusions (if an argument has more than one conclusion)
- **phenomenon** (event): any observable behavior or occurrence
- **premise** (reason/fact/support): evidence offered to prove a conclusion
- **problem**: a conflict or situation that needs a solution
- **proposal** (suggestion/recommendation): a course of action that someone is supporting
- **proposition**: a sentence (in arguments, a premise or conclusion)
- **reason** (fact/support/premise): evidence offered to prove a conclusion
- **recommendation** (proposal/suggestion): a course of action that someone is supporting
- **solution**: an answer to a problem
- **suggestion** (recommendation/proposal): a course of action that someone is supporting
- **support** (premise/reason/fact): evidence offered to prove a conclusion

Patterns of Reasoning

Patterns of reasoning can also be thought of as types of arguments. Most arguments made in life are not absolutely, conclusively valid. For example, you might argue as follows:

> **Premise:** Mike is ten minutes late to the meeting.
>
> **Premise:** He has never been late to meetings that he knows about.
>
> **Conclusion:** So, I bet he did not know about the meeting.

Your conclusion is that Mike did not know about the meeting. This conclusion may very well be true; after all, Mike is never late, and now he is ten minutes late. But is it certain? No. Why not? Because today might be the first time Mike is late to a meeting that he knows about.

If we knew more about the situation, we might be able to say with greater certainty whether the conclusion of this argument ("Mike did not know about the meeting") is likely or unlikely; but as it stands, the argument is not conclusive.

This is an example of **inductive reasoning** (also called **informal logic**). In this sort of argument, you can potentially bring in new, or additional, information to prove or disprove the conclusion. It is called inductive logic because you can *induce*, or bring in, more premises to evaluate the conclusion.

The Ford Focus argument is an inductive argument, and we practiced adding in additional premises to strengthen or weaken it. We do not technically refer to inductive arguments as valid or invalid; instead, we refer to them as strong or weak. The LSAT will ask you to strengthen or weaken inductive arguments in the Logical Reasoning sections.

Deductive reasoning, on the other hand, exists where your conclusion follows directly and conclusively from your premises, with 100 percent certainty. For example:

> **Premise**: If Mike had remembered the meeting, he would have been here early.
>
> **Premise**: But he is late.
>
> **Conclusion**: So, Mike must not have remembered the meeting.

Given the premises, the conclusion is certain. This argument is a deductive argument. It is called deductive logic because you can deduce, or figure out, the conclusion directly from the premises without looking elsewhere. There is no way to strengthen or weaken the argument. When an argument is this strong, it is called **valid**. Arguments that attempt to be valid deductive arguments but use faulty reasoning (explained below) are called **invalid**.

Now, you might be thinking, "But what if Mike had car trouble? Or what if he just decided to sleep in? Just because he is late, how can you say it is certain that Mike did not remember the meeting?" The reason this argument is still perfectly valid is that our premise states "*If Mike had remembered the meeting*, he would have been here early." Based on this premise, we know with certainty that Mike would have been early if he had remembered the meeting.

Maybe you disagree with this premise, but your disagreement is a factual challenge to the argument, not a logical challenge. On the LSAT, your task is never to dispute the facts (premises) presented; your task is only to evaluate the logical soundness of the conclusions that are supposed to follow from those facts. Even if the LSAT states, "The moon is made of green cheese" as a premise in an argument, your thought should not be, "No, it isn't." Just worry about the logic in the argument.

Diagramming

Table 1.3 defines some common symbols in diagramming logical arguments.

TABLE 1.3. Symbols Used in Diagramming Logical Arguments

SYMBOL	MEANING	EXAMPLE
→	if...then	A → B (If A is true, then B is true.)
~	not	~A (A is not true/A is false.)
∴	therefore	∴ A (Therefore, A is true.)

As you work through LSAT problems, you may find it useful to diagram some of the logical arguments in the passages, especially conditional statements ("if...then" statements).

For example, take the statement "If life as we know it exists, then there must be water." You might denote this simply as

$$L \to W$$

Here, L stands for "Life as we know it exists," and W stands for "There is water." The arrow (→) denotes the "if...then" relationship: "If L is true, then W must also be true."

Students often diagram the sentence, "If life as we know it exists, then there must be water" as "L = W." But this is incorrect. The statement "L = W" could easily be confused with "W = L."

Our conditional statement, however, only goes in one direction ("if life, then water"); it does *not* mean "If there is water, then there is life." That is why we use a one-directional arrow to convey conditions: "L → W" just means if there is life, then there is water. It is not the same as "W → L."

The LSAT will test your ability to understand and apply conditional statements correctly. In Analytical Reasoning questions (Logic Games), you will have to read statements like "Nancy performs third only if Larry performs fifth," and then apply reasoning correctly. If Nancy performs third, then Larry performs fifth. But just because Larry performs fifth does not mean Nancy performs third. We will look more into this, as well as how conditional statements frequently appear in logical reasoning passages, in the next few pages.

If you find yourself facing several conditional statements in a complex argument, diagramming the argument in the margin can be a useful tool to help you understand what the author is trying to convey. Using shorthand is useful for saving time as you do this—and for focusing on the structure of the argument rather than the details of what is being said.

HELPFUL HINT

Do not use an equal sign (=) to represent a conditional statement.

Formal Logic (Deductive Reasoning)

Mixed Hypothetical Arguments

Here we have provided two common valid patterns of reasoning, as well as two common invalid patterns of reasoning. These are called **mixed hypothetical arguments** because they all take a hypothetical (if...then) statement and apply it to an actual situation.

TABLE 1.4. Mixed Hypothetical Arguments

VALID (POSITIVE) ARGUMENT

Pattern:

If A is true, then B is true.

A is true.

Therefore, B is true.

Shorthand:

A → B

A

∴ B

Example:

If the car is running, then it has gasoline.

This car is running.

Therefore, this car has gasoline.

(This is a perfectly valid deductive argument.)

Invalid (Mistaken Reversal)

Pattern:

If A is true, then B is true.

B is true.

Therefore, A is true.

Shorthand:

A → B

B

∴ A

Example:

If the car is running, then it has gasoline.

This car has gasoline.

Therefore, this car is running.

This argument is fatally flawed. Gasoline is necessary for the car to run. However, just because the car has gasoline does not ensure that the car *will* run. For example, the car might have a faulty battery. This argument assumes that "If the car is running, then it has gas" is the same as "If the car has gas, then it is running." This is always flawed logic.

In abstract (pattern) terms, this argument wrongly assumes that "If A then B" is the same as "If B then A." This is always flawed logic.

See the mistaken reversal discussion for more information.

VALID (CONTRAPOSITIVE) ARGUMENT

Pattern:

If A is true, then B is true.

B is false.

Therefore, A is false.

Shorthand:

A → B

~B

∴ ~A

Example:

If the car is running, then it has gasoline.

This car is out of gas.

Therefore, this car is not running.

(This is a perfectly valid deductive argument.)

Invalid (Mistaken Negation)

Pattern:

If A is true, then B is true.

A is false.

Therefore, B is false.

Shorthand:

A → B

~A

∴ ~B

Example:

If the car is running, then it has gasoline.

This car is not running.

Therefore, this car is out of gas.

This argument is fatally flawed. If the car is running, this is sufficient to ensure that the car has gasoline. However, the fact that the car is not running does not necessitate that it is out of gas. Perhaps it has a faulty battery or a missing engine. This argument assumes that "If the car is running, then it has gas" is the same as "If the car is not running, then it is out of gas." This is always flawed logic.

In abstract (pattern) terms, this argument wrongly assumes that "If A then B" is the same as "If no A, then no B." This is always flawed logic.

See the mistaken negation discussion for more information.

The LSAT tests your ability to recognize these and other common patterns of reasoning. In some cases, you will be given two of an argument's three components, and your task will be to come up with an answer that provides the third component in such a way as to complete a valid argument.

The valid, positive argument form in Table 1.4 is very common. Consider the following examples:

> **Premise**: If you work hard, you will succeed. $W \rightarrow S$
>
> **Premise**: Bob works hard. W
>
> **Conclusion**: Therefore, Bob will succeed. $\therefore S$
>
> **Premise**: You cannot travel to Mexico if you do not have a passport. $\sim P \rightarrow \sim T$
>
> **Premise**: Jerry does not have a passport. $\sim P$
>
> **Conclusion**: Therefore, Jerry cannot travel to Mexico. $\therefore \sim T$

Note that the "if...then" statement in premise 1 here is essentially "If no passport, then no travel." Pay careful attention to where the "if" falls in conditional statements. Also note that premise 1 is still a conditional statement, even though it does not explicitly use "if...then." The conditional relationship is "If good grades, then study." According to this statement, without studying, it is impossible to get good grades; thus, this is a perfectly valid argument.

Note that these are *not* circular arguments. The first premise of each argument is a purely hypothetical statement that tells us what would happen *if* some condition were to come true. Then, the second premise tells us about an actual situation where that condition actually does come true. Based on those premises, we are able to draw our conclusion about this actual situation.

The valid, contrapositive argument form is also very common. Consider these examples:

> **Premise**: To get good grades, you must study. $G \rightarrow S$
>
> **Premise**: Carol refuses to study. $\sim S$
>
> **Conclusion**: Therefore, Carol will not get good grades. $\therefore \sim G$
>
> **Premise**: If you are eligible to vote, you must be eighteen or older. $E \rightarrow 18$
>
> **Premise**: Jonathan is seventeen. ~ 18
>
> **Conclusion**: Therefore, Jonathan is not eligible to vote. $\therefore \sim E$

If you are wondering what all this diagramming is about, realize that every argument you have ever made follows some pattern of reasoning.

Even our example "Oh, you are bleeding... you must need a bandage" follows the valid, positive form of argumentation:

> **Premise**: If you're bleeding, you need a bandage.
>
> **Premise**: You're bleeding.
>
> **Conclusion**: So, you must need a bandage.

As previously noted, you would probably never say the unstated "if...then" premise, but you are still using this pattern of reasoning. The LSAT tests your ability to recognize and make convincing arguments, skills that you will need both in law school and in your future as an advocate.

Disjunctive Argument (Either-Or)

While the preceding mixed hypothetical arguments are the most common patterns of deductive reasoning on the LSAT, Tables 1.5 through 1.7 show a few other patterns that you are likely to encounter. (Note: the disjunctive argument is a valid argument; do not confuse it with the invalid either-or fallacy.)

TABLE 1.5. Disjunctive Arguments (Either-Or)

PATTERN	SHORTHAND	EXAMPLE
Either A is true or B is true.	A or B	Everyone must take either Spanish or French.
A is false.	~A	Cheryl is not taking Spanish.
Therefore, B is true.	∴ B	Therefore, Cheryl is taking French.

TABLE 1.6. Pure Hypothetical Argument

PATTERN	SHORTHAND	EXAMPLE
If A is true, then B is true.	A →B	If it is a dog, then it is a mammal.
If B is true, then C is true.	B →C	If it is a mammal, then it has hair.
So, if A is true, then C is true.	∴ A → C	So, if it is a dog, then it has hair.

TABLE 1.7. Constructive Dilemma

PATTERN	SHORTHAND	EXAMPLE
If A is true, then B is true.	A → B	If I go to law school, then I will be a lawyer.
If C is true, then D is true.	C →D	If I go to medical school, then I will be a doctor.
Either A is true or C is true.	A or C	I am going to either law school or medical school.
So, either B is true or D is true.	∴ B or D	So, I will be either a lawyer or a doctor.

The variations in Table 1.8 are all mixed hypothetical patterns of reasoning, but they involve more premises than the simple positive and contrapositive forms. In theory, no limit exists for the number of premises that you can have in an argument, although LSAT Logical Reasoning passages do not usually support conclusions with more than five premises.

As noted earlier, the LSAT frequently tests your ability to fill in missing links in order to turn partial arguments into complete arguments that follow patterns.

TABLE 1.8. Mixed Hypothetical Patterns of Reasoning

PATTERN	SHORTHAND	EXAMPLE
If A is true, then B is true.	A → B	If it is a dog, then it is a mammal.
If B is true, then C is true.	B → C	If it is a mammal, then it has hair.
A is true.	A	Fido is a dog.
Therefore, C is true.	∴ C	Therefore, Fido has hair.
If A is true, then B is true.	A → B	If you are a lawyer, you went to law school.
If B is true, then C is true.	B → C	If you went to law school, you took the LSAT.
C is not true.	~C	Ashley never took the LSAT.
Therefore, A is not true.	∴ ~A	Therefore, Ashley is not a lawyer.
If A is true, then B is true.	A → B	If you are a lawyer, you went to law school.
If B is true, then C is true.	B → C	If you went to law school, you did well on the LSAT.
If D is not true, then C is not true.	~D → ~C, or C → D	If you did not know how to tell apart patterns of reasoning, you would not have done well on the LSAT.
A is true.	A	Ashley is a lawyer.
Therefore, D is true. As discussed later, ~D → ~C is the same as C → D.	∴ D	Therefore, Ashley knows how to tell apart patterns of reasoning.

Conditional Statements

So far, we have dealt with conditional statements mostly in their "if…then" forms. On the LSAT, you will see conditional statements in a variety of forms. For example, consider the following statements:

1. If it is an animal, then it is mortal.
2. If it is not mortal, then it is not an animal.
3. Only if it is mortal is it an animal.
4. It is not an animal unless it is mortal.
5. It must be mortal or else it is not an animal.
6. Either it is mortal or it is not an animal.
7. It is mortal if it is an animal.
8. Only mortals are animals.
9. It is an animal only if it is mortal.
10. All animals are mortals.

11. No animals fail to be mortal.

12. Being an animal is sufficient for being a mortal.

13. Being a mortal is necessary for being an animal.

Hopefully, as you read these statements, you noticed that all thirteen sentences express the exact same condition, with absolutely zero variation in meaning. You should note that *none* of these statements says "If it is mortal, then it is an animal" or any variation on that sentence, which would be a mistaken reversal. Here is another conditional statement expressed all thirteen ways:

1. If you get a 170 or higher on the LSAT, then you studied hard.

2. If you do not study hard, then you will not get a 170 or higher on the LSAT.

3. Only if you study hard will you get a 170 or higher on the LSAT.

4. You will not get a 170 or higher on the LSAT unless you study hard.

5. You must study hard or else you will not get a 170 or higher on the LSAT.

6. Either you study hard or you do not get a 170 or higher on the LSAT.

7. You studied hard if you got a 170 or higher on the LSAT.

8. Only those who study hard get 170 or higher on the LSAT.

9. You get a 170 or higher on the LSAT only if you study hard.

10. All 170+ scorers studied hard.

11. No 170+ scorer fails to study hard.

12. Scoring 170 or higher on the LSAT is sufficient to assert that you studied hard.

13. Studying hard is necessary for scoring 170 or higher on the LSAT.

In shorthand, here are the same thirteen forms. All of these mean "A → B" and its equivalent "~B → ~A."

1. If A is true, then B is true.

2. If B is false, then A is false.

3. Only if B is true is A true.

4. A cannot be true unless B is true.

5. B must be true or else A is false.

6. Either B is true or A is false.

7. B is true if A is true. (Again, notice where the "if" is. This is *not* saying "If B then A.")

8. Only B is A.

9. A only if B.

10. All A is B.

11. No A fails to be B.

12. A is sufficient for B. (Or, A ensures B.)

13. B is necessary for A. (Or, A requires B.)

 HELPFUL HINT

Recognize that no matter the values of A and B in your conditional statement, you can rearrange the sentence into any of these thirteen forms without changing the meaning of the statement. Just be careful not to confuse any form of "If A, then B" with any form of "If B, then A."

IF A, THEN B

"If A, then B" is usually the easiest form for working with conditional statements. The phrase *If A, then B* is clearer than *A only if B* or *No A unless B*, even though all these forms have the same meaning.

As you spot conditional statements (on any section of the LSAT), process the statement and articulate it to yourself in "If A then B" form. Thus, on test day this statement is diagrammed as "A → B."

Also, when you see "if" in the middle of a sentence, you should start reading the sentence from "if":

> "The lawn will get wet *if* it rains."
>
> Read this sentence as: "*If* it rains, the lawn will get wet."

Just be careful not to read the sentence as "If the lawn gets wet, then it rained." That would change the meaning of the sentence entirely.

ONLY IF

"Only if" is *not* the same as "if." Consider the difference between the following two sentences:

1. The dog barks if there is an intruder.
2. The dog barks only if there is an intruder.

We could read sentence 1 as "If there is an intruder, then the dog barks." (This is the conditional statement that we learned immediately prior: I → B.)

Sentence 2, however, says that the only way the dog barks is when there is an intruder: "If the dog barks, there is an intruder." On test day, we will diagram this conditional statement as "B → I."

In sentence 1, knowing that there is an intruder guarantees that the dog is barking. However, other things might also make the dog bark. In fact, this dog may always be barking.

In sentence 2, knowing that the dog is barking guarantees that there is an intruder. However, just because there is an intruder does not mean this dog will bark. In fact, this dog may never bark, even if there are intruders present.

Be sure to understand the difference. Sentence 1 says that the presence of an intruder is sufficient for the dog to bark. Sentence 2 says that the presence of an intruder is necessary for the dog to bark. Changing the "if" to "only if" changes the subsequent condition from a sufficient condition to a necessary condition.

As you read sentences in the form "A is true only if B is true," you should mentally reword them as "If A is true, then B is true."

IF AND ONLY IF

A speaker may want to express the idea that the dog barks when there is an intruder, *and* that when the dog barks, we know there is an intruder. That is where a sentence like this comes in: "The dog barks if, *and only if*, there is an intruder."

This is really just a combination of sentences 1 and 2 above. When you encounter "if and only if" (or "if but only if") statements on the LSAT, you should treat them accordingly. "If A is true, then B is true" and "If B is true, then A is true." On test day, this statement is diagrammed as "A ←→ B." That said, these sorts of statements appear rather infrequently on the LSAT. A common source of confusion is how we use conditional statements in real life.

Often, when someone says, "My dog only barks if there is an intruder," they mean two things:

1. My dog will not bark if there is not an intruder (i.e., My dog barks only if there is an intruder).

2. My dog barks if there is an intruder (i.e., If there is an intruder, my dog barks).

Rarely will someone actually take the time to say in real life, "My dog barks if, and only if, there is an intruder." Be aware of how you use conditional statements in your own life. If you use "if" statements to mean "if and only if," then consider changing your ways. Think about the confusion that might arise from these examples:

1. Father to son: "You can have dessert if you clean your room."

    In this example, even if the son *does not* clean his room, he might still be able to have dessert. The father should not say this if he wants to *require* his son to clean his room in order to have dessert. Instead, he could say, "You can have dessert if, and only if, you clean your room." As written in sentence 1, all the father has done is guaranteed that the son can have dessert if he cleans his room; he has not said what happens if the son does not clean his room.

2. Academic policy: "Students graduate if they complete 120 credit hours."

    In this example, the school guarantees students that completing 120 credit hours results in graduation. However, what if the school has other requirements, such as a minimum GPA? The way this sentence is written, there are no other requirements for graduation; all we know is that attaining 120 credit hours ensures graduation. If the school wanted 120 credit hours to be a requirement (while allowing for the possibility of other requirements), the policy should say, "Students graduate only if they complete 120 credit hours."

3. Postal employee: "The letter will arrive tomorrow if you use express mail."

    In this example, the postal employee says that using express mail will guarantee delivery tomorrow. However, this does not exclude the possibility that other forms of mail will also result in delivery tomorrow. If the postal employee wanted to convey that there is no other way for the letter to arrive tomorrow, he should have said, "The letter will arrive tomorrow if, and only if, you use express mail."

UNLESS

Consider the examples:

- You cannot drive unless you have a driver's license.

- You cannot vote unless you are eighteen or older.
- You will succeed in life unless you become selfish.

These would be expressed in "if...then" form as follows:

> If you can drive, you have a driver's license.
>
> *or*
>
> If you do not have a driver's license, you cannot drive.
>
> If you can vote, you are eighteen or older.
>
> *or*
>
> If you are not eighteen or older, you cannot vote.
>
> If you do not become selfish, you will succeed in life.
>
> *or*
>
> If you do not succeed in life, you have become selfish.

There are two lessons here.

First, any conditional form in the phrase *A is not true unless B is true* is identical to *If A is true, then B is true*. Similarly, the phrase *A is true unless B is true* is identical to *If A is not true, then B is true*. Second, *unless* essentially means "if not." Thus, you could rephrase sentence 3 as follows:

> You will succeed in life unless you become selfish. (Original)
>
> You will succeed in life if you do not become selfish. (Rephrased)
>
> If you do not become selfish, you will succeed in life. (Rephrased, and starting with *if*)

DID YOU KNOW?

"Unless" is a word that even highly educated individuals misuse on a regular basis. Consider this statement: "We will not hire another employee unless we double our sales." You might think this means that if we double our sales, we will hire another employee, but that is a mistaken reversal. All we know is that if we do not double our sales, we will not hire another employee.

TABLE 1.9. Recap of Diagrams

CONDITIONAL STATEMENT	EXAMPLE	DIAGRAM ON TEST DAY	NOTES
if A, then B	If Jake eats a slice of key lime pie, he will be full.	P → F	Remember, eating a slice of key lime pie is *sufficient but not necessary* for Jake to be full. Hypothetically, Jake could also be full by eating a brownie or ice cream sundae.
only if	Only if Jake eats a slice of key lime pie will he be full.	F → P	Now, eating a slice of key lime pie is the only way that Jake can be full. Thus, eating a slice of key lime pie is a *necessary condition* for Jake to be full.
if and only if	If and only if Jake eats a slice of key lime pie will he be full.	P ←→ F	Now, if Jake eats a slice of key lime pie, he will be full, *and* only if Jake eats a slice of key lime pie will he be full. Now, eating a slice of key lime pie is both a *necessary* and a *sufficient condition* for Jake's fullness.

Disproving Conditional Statements

To disprove the statement "If A is true, then B is true," it is not good enough to show that A is false. Take, for example, "If the moon were made of green cheese, then it would smell bad." You cannot disprove this statement by proving that the moon is not made of green cheese. To disprove the statement, you would need to show that (1) the moon is made of green cheese, and (2) it does not smell bad. This is a fundamental principle of logic:

To disprove "If A is true, then B is true," you must show "A is true. (And) B is false."

Sufficient Conditions and Necessary Conditions

We have already mentioned sufficient conditions and necessary conditions. These are important terms that the LSAT will use in Logical Reasoning answer choices, and you should master the relationship between a sufficient condition and a necessary condition.

By definition, when we say "If A, then B," we are designating A as a sufficient condition for B, and B as a necessary condition for A. Remember these are equivalent forms:

1. If A is true, then B is true.
2. A is sufficient for B.
3. A ensures B.
4. A requires B.
5. B is necessary for A.

This is true for *any* "if...then" statement. For example, "If you are making pancakes, then you have flour." Using these five variations, we could say the following:

1. If you are making pancakes, then you have flour.
2. That you are making pancakes is sufficient to assert that you have flour.
3. That you are making pancakes ensures that you have flour.
4. Making pancakes requires flour.
5. Flour is necessary for making pancakes.

Observe the relationship here. "Making pancakes" is the sufficient condition, and "flour" is the necessary condition.

Again, watch out for mistaken reversals and mistaken negations. These fallacies occur when someone wrongly assumes that a necessary condition is really a sufficient condition. The following is a mistaken reversal:

Premise: If you are making pancakes, then you have flour.

Premise: Jim has flour.

Conclusion: So, Jim must be making pancakes.

This wrongly assumes that flour (a necessary condition for making pancakes, according to our first premise) is a sufficient condition for making pancakes. In factual terms, we would say that just because Jim has flour, it does not mean he is making pancakes.

Finally, consider the examples in Table 1.10 in terms of sufficient and necessary conditions.

TABLE 1.10. Sufficient and Necessary Conditions

CONDITIONAL STATEMENT	SUFFICIENT CONDITION	NECESSARY CONDITION
You cannot drive unless you have a license.	driving	driver's license
You cannot vote unless you are eighteen or older.	voting	being eighteen or older
You will succeed unless you become selfish.	not succeeding	becoming selfish
My dog barks only if there is an intruder.	dog barking	intruder
My dog barks if there is an intruder.	intruder	dog barking

Categorical Formal Logic
ALL, SOME, AND NONE STATEMENTS

So far, we have looked at deductive arguments that primarily use conditional statements (if, only if, unless, etc.). However, not all deductive arguments use conditional statements. Some use statements with "all," "some," or "none." For example:

Premise: All plants are green.

Premise: Some plants are decorative objects.

Conclusion: Therefore, some decorative objects are green.

This is a valid argument, and it follows this pattern:

Premise: All A is B.

Premise: Some A is C.

Conclusion: Therefore, some C is B.
(Note: "Some B is C" would be equivalent here.)

Sometimes, it is useful to visualize all/some/none statements. We can see that this argument is valid by drawing out the premises. Figure 1.1 shows how you might visualize the first premise ("All plants are green"):

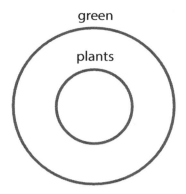

Figure 1.1. "All Plants Are Green"

It becomes clear from the diagram that every plant is contained within the set of things that are green.

Figure 1.2 draws in the second premise ("Some plants are decorative objects"):

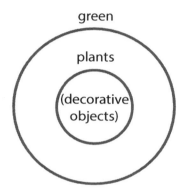

Figure 1.2. "Some Plants Are Decorative Objects"

Note that you should not diagram the conclusion, only the premises of the argument presented. Then look at the diagram to see if the premises provided are sufficient to prove the conclusion. If the argument is valid, then you should be able to draw just the premises, and the conclusion should be apparent from your drawing, as a logical consequence of the premises.

What about in this case? Our conclusion was that some decorative objects are green. Looking at Figure 1.2, it is apparent that some decorative objects must indeed be green, thus proving that this is a valid pattern of reasoning.

An important note: in the Figure 1.2, notice how "decorative objects" is written in parentheses. This is because our sentence was *some* plants are decorative objects. We are not saying that all decorative objects are plants. If we wanted to say that, we would write "decorative objects" inside of another circle that is *entirely within* "plants." Instead, writing "(decorative objects)" indicates that there are *some* decorative objects that are plants, without ruling out the possibility that there are also decorative objects that are not plants. To denote

"Some A is B," write A inside of B in a different way than you would write to denote "All A is B."

"ALL" STATEMENTS AND "IF" STATEMENTS

Note that using a visual diagram, such as the circles, is helpful for diagramming arguments that contain "some" statements; after all, you cannot effectively use the arrow (→) to represent a sentence like "Some plants are decorative objects."

However, if your argument just contains "all" statements, consider how these statements are similar to "if…then" statements. For example, the following two arguments are essentially the same:

Premise: All humans are mortal.   **Premise**: If human, then mortal.

Premise: This man is human.   **Premise**: This man is human.

Conclusion: So, this man is mortal.   **Conclusion**: So, this man is mortal.

You could diagram both of these arguments in one of two ways:

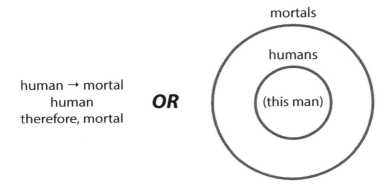

Figure 1.3. "All" and "If" Statements

Diagramming "if…then" statements tends to be easier than diagramming a bunch of concentric circles in complex passages. When you see an "all" statement, it might be helpful to turn it into an "if…then" statement, so you can look for possible patterns of reasoning that follow our conditional reasoning patterns. However, if your argument has "some" statements, you are probably better off visualizing the argument with either a diagram like our circles or a Venn diagram, depending on your preference.

NO/NONE STATEMENTS

Examine the following statement: "No advanced society fails to take care of its elderly."

Some readers will interpret this statement as "If you are not an advanced society, then you fail to take care of your elderly." But this is wrong.

This statement is really saying "All advanced societies do take care of their elderly." Rewriting this statement in "if…then" terms results in "If a society is advanced, then it takes care of its elderly," not "If a society is not advanced, then it does not take care of its elderly." The latter is a mistaken negation.

Here is the transformation process for reading a "no" statement more directly: Start with "No advanced society fails to take care of its elderly."

Process the "no": "Advanced societies do not fail to take care of their elderly." Remove the double negative: "Advanced societies take care of their elderly."

Some additional examples (equivalent forms) appear in Table 1.11.

TABLE 1.11. Equivalent Forms		
NO/NONE STATEMENT	**ALL STATEMENT**	**"IF...THEN" STATEMENT**
No apes can talk.	All apes are incapable of talking.	If it is an ape, then it cannot talk.
None of the chairs are blue.	All of the chairs are not blue.	If it is a chair, then it is not blue.
No fried foods are healthy.	All fried foods are unhealthy.	If it is a fried food, then it is unhealthy.
None of the candidates has any experience.	All of the candidates lack experience.	If a candidate, then no experience.

Numbers

Many people get confused by the LSAT's use of words like "some," "few," "many," and "most." These words seem vague, but they do have consistent definitions.

Some means "one or more"—*not* "more than one." If you say, "Some of the books on the shelf are green," you are saying, "There is one or more green books on the shelf." Even though you say, "some green books," using the plural form of *books*, you are not actually saying that there are *two* or more green books. Consider what you have to do to disprove someone who makes a "some" statement:

> Person 1: "Some of the books on the shelf are green."
>
> You: "That's not true. There are *no* green books on the shelf." Here, your counterargument is effective. But consider this:
>
> Person 1: "Some of the books on the shelf are green."
>
> You: "That's not true. There is one green book on the shelf."

Here, your counterargument is not effective. You have not disproved person 1, because you have not shown that there are no green books on the shelf.

Also note that saying "Some of the books on the shelf are green" *does not* imply that some of the books on the shelf are *not* green. It may be the case that all of the books on the shelf are green. Even so, it would still be true that some books on the shelf are green.

Most means "more than half." If you have one hundred students, *most* students would be fifty-one or more. If you have ten students, *most* would be at least six. Consider this argument:

> **Premise**: Most French majors are familiar with Latin.
>
> **Premise**: Most French majors are well versed in poetry.
>
> **Conclusion**: Therefore, some people who are familiar with Latin are well versed in poetry.

This is a valid argument. If we pretend that there are one hundred French majors, then there must be at least fifty-one who are familiar with Latin, and fifty-one who are well versed in poetry. Even if we try to minimize the amount of overlap between those who are familiar with Latin and those who are well versed in poetry, there will still be some overlap, so the conclusion follows with 100 percent certainty that some people who are familiar with Latin are well versed in poetry.

Few and *many* are relative to each other. *Few* means "less than many." *Many* means "more than a few."

You may think those are ridiculous definitions, but consider how we use the term *many*. If we are talking about grains of rice, is ten enough to qualify as "many"? Probably not. One hundred would probably not count as "many." But if we are talking about elephants, three elephants could be many elephants. *Many* is a relative term, depending on the object it modifies. It is fair to assume that *many* means "at least two." However, be careful with the phrase *too many*. As you well know, sometimes even one of a thing can be too many. It all depends upon context.

Few is also a relative term. A few blood cells could mean hundreds of blood cells, while a few skyscrapers may mean one or two. When you see *few*, it is best to treat it like *some* and note that it is simply smaller than *many*.

All and *not all* are opposites. The argument "All plants are green" could be disproved by the simple statement "Not all plants are green." "Not all" does not mean that *no* plants are green, after all, so the counterargument is valid. This makes extreme statements like "All plants are green" very difficult to support; the burden of proof for defeating such arguments is very low. On the contrary, the burden of proof for defeating statements like "Some plants are green" is much higher, since you would have to show that every single plant in existence is not green.

Extreme Language in LSAT Arguments

A fundamental principle of logic is that your conclusion cannot be stronger than the premises supporting it. For example, consider this flawed argument:

> **Premise**: Larry and Ted smoke two packs a day and stay in excellent health.
>
> **Conclusion**: So, most people could smoke two packs a day and stay in excellent health.

The problem with this argument is that it uses a premise about two people to support a broad conclusion about most people. Just because something is true of two people does not mean it will apply generally. For LSAT questions asking what must be true, choose answers whose truth is 100 percent certain, based on the given information.

Table 1.12 lists common modifiers, organized from extreme to modest.

TABLE 1.12. Common Modifiers		
EXTREME	**MODERATE**	**MODEST**
every/everyone	most	some
any	all	few
all	—	not all
none	—	—
only	—	—
always	often	sometimes
never	seldom, rarely	—
will	tends to/generally	may
must	probably	can
—	likely	could
should/ought to	—	—

Remember, your premises should be at least as strong as your conclusion. It is okay if your premise is stronger than your conclusion, but you cannot make a sound argument if your conclusion is more extreme than your premises.

PRACTICE QUESTIONS

Each statement means either "B → I" or "I → B." None of the statements are ambiguous. None of the statements mean more than one of these two conditional expressions.

1. For each of the conditional statements below,
   - diagram the statement as "B → I" if it is equivalent in meaning to "If the dog is barking, then there is an intruder."
   - diagram the statement as "I → B" if it is equivalent in meaning to "If there is an intruder, then the dog is barking."

Conditional Statement   Your Diagram

A) The dog does not fail to bark when there is an intruder.

B) Either there is an intruder or the dog is not barking.

C) There cannot be an intruder unless the dog barks.

Conditional Statement	Your Diagram

D) There must be an intruder in order for the dog to bark.

E) The dog cannot bark unless there is an intruder.

F) Either the dog is barking or there is no intruder.

G) The presence of an intruder requires that the dog barks.

H) If the dog is not barking, then there is no intruder.

I) There is an intruder only if the dog barks.

J) The dog barks only if there is an intruder.

K) If there is no intruder, then the dog is not barking.

L) If the dog barks, then there is an intruder.

M) The presence of an intruder ensures that the dog barks.

N) The dog's barking ensures that there is an intruder.

O) The dog's barking is sufficient to assert that there is an intruder.

P) There is an intruder if the dog barks.

Q) The dog's barking requires that there is an intruder.

R) The dog must bark for there to be an intruder.

S) The dog barks if there is an intruder.

T) Only if there is an intruder does the dog bark.

U) Only if the dog is barking is there an intruder.

V) The presence of an intruder is sufficient to assert that the dog barks.

W) The dog must be barking or else there would not be an intruder.

2. Rewrite the following conditional statements in "if...then" form.

A) Completing law school requires lots of reading.

B) Mark will not become a Supreme Court clerk unless he develops better interviewing skills.

C) In order to be elected, Griswold must change his rhetoric.

D) The tide must have come in, or else she would be selling seashells on the seashore.

E) Whales are mammals.

F) Only mammals are whales.

G) Slovakia will only refrain from invading Poland in the event of rapid economic improvement.

H) Meteors could not have killed the dinosaurs unless debris is fatal.

I) Only ham and cheese sandwiches are available for five dollars from Jimmy John's.

J) My cell phone will ring only if I forgot to turn it on silent.

K) Lindsey must have eaten too many hot peppers, or she would not be suffering from acid reflux.

Informal Logic (Inductive Reasoning)

As mentioned earlier, informal logic (inductive reasoning) is used in any argument that can be strengthened or weakened by bringing in additional premises. In the sections that follow, the patterns of reasoning discussed will generally occur in inductive arguments.

For a thorough analysis of an inductive argument, please review the Ford Focus example.

You should recognize that you can turn an inductive argument into a deductive argument by adding a sufficient assumption that guarantees the argument's conclusion. Once you have guaranteed the argument's conclusion with 100 percent certainty, there is nothing you can do to make the conclusion any stronger or weaker. This, by definition, would be a deductive argument.

At first glance, these logical concepts may seem foreign. Consider, though, that you already use inductive and deductive reasoning on a regular basis. You simply did not know that the way in which you argued was called "inductive." Take charge of the language and logic that you use on a daily basis; become so fluent in the concepts laid out here that you can easily explain them to a peer.

You will find that improving on the LSAT is a matter of practice, experience, and familiarity. This is not a test for which you can cram a lot of information and hope to do well. Rather, you improve on the LSAT by confronting your mistakes one at a time, examining your thought process, and recalibrating your logical processes so that you will not make the same mistakes in the future. Improving on the LSAT is a lot like learning a language: memorizing flash cards is nearly useless, while actually learning how the grammar and structure of the language works (through immersion or textbook learning) is far more effective.

Condition, Correlation, and Causation

Do not confuse correlation with causation. This trap is all over the LSAT, and you should learn to watch out for it. Consider this situation:

> **Proposition 1:** Jordan drinks coffee on Mondays.
>
> **Proposition 2:** Jordan gets headaches on Mondays.

Here, we have an example of a **correlation** between two things: coffee and Jordan's headaches. We say these two things are correlated because they happen together; the incidence of Jordan's headaches is related to the incidence of Jordan's coffee drinking. Other examples of correlations include "Crime tends to be higher in low-income neighborhoods" (here, crime and poverty are correlated), or "Rugby players generally weigh more than average" (here, weight and playing rugby are correlated).

Just because two things are correlated, however, does not mean that one of those things causes the other. For example:

> **Premise**: Jordan drinks coffee on Mondays.
>
> **Premise**: Jordan gets headaches on Mondays.
>
> **Conclusion**: Therefore, coffee causes Jordan's headaches.

You will see arguments like this over and over again on the LSAT. They are all flawed. Based on the correlation between coffee and Jordan's headaches, there are several possibilities:

1. Coffee causes Jordan's headaches.
2. Headaches cause Jordan to drink coffee.
3. A third factor causes Jordan to get headaches *and* to drink coffee.
4. It is coincidental that Jordan drinks coffee and gets headaches on the same day (that is, some factor causes Jordan to drink coffee, and some other, unrelated factor causes his headaches).

On the LSAT, it is common to immediately assume that the first possibility is true, without first stopping to rule out other possibilities. This is a problem, because if all we have to go on is the correlation, we really do not know that coffee causes Jordan's headaches. Perhaps Jordan gets headaches every Monday and then drinks coffee to cure them. Or, perhaps Jordan stays out late on Sunday nights, resulting in a headache and the need to drink coffee the next morning. These are all possibilities. Of course, it is also possible that one factor causes Jordan to drink coffee, and a different factor causes Jordan to get headaches. This would be an example of coincidence.

Here's how you would argue **causation** based on a correlation:

> **Premise**: Jordan drinks coffee on Mondays.
>
> **Premise**: Jordan gets headaches on Mondays.
>
> **Premise**: Nothing else other than coffee could plausibly cause Jordan's headaches.
>
> **Conclusion**: Therefore, coffee causes Jordan's headaches.

Thus, given a correlation between two factors X and Y, these are the possibilities:

1. X causes Y.
2. Y causes X.
3. There is a common cause of both X and Y.
4. One factor (A) causes X, and another factor (B) causes Y (coincidence).

If the first possibility is your conclusion, you would strengthen this conclusion by ruling out possibilities 2 – 4; "Nothing else could cause Y" is a broad statement, and does well. Similarly, you would weaken this conclusion by adding in any one of possibilities 2 – 4. In an argument flaw question, you would point out that an argument concluding any one of these possibilities "fails to consider the possibility that" one of the others is true. Keep this in mind as you complete Logical Reasoning sections: cause-and-effect arguments should be a red flag that makes you look for correlation-causation confusion.

Note that correlation and causation are both distinct from **condition**. A conditional statement would be "If Jordan has a headache, then he has drunk coffee." This is different from causation, because this statement does not tell us whether headaches cause Jordan to drink coffee or vice versa. As we discussed earlier, all this sentence tells us is that Jordan's headache is a sufficient condition to assert that Jordan has drunk coffee, and that drinking coffee is a necessary condition for asserting that Jordan has a headache. Do not assume from a conditional statement like "If A, then B" that A causes B.

These are independent concepts:

> If there was a flood, then it rained a lot. ≠
> The flood caused it to rain a lot.
>
> If the dog barked, then there was an intruder. ≠
> The dog's bark caused there to be an intruder.

The following set of examples illustrates the difference between correlation, condition, and causation:

> **Correlation:** Competitive parents tend to have more aggressive children than collaborative parents.
>
> **Condition:** If parents are competitive, then their children will be aggressive.
>
> **Causation:** Competitive parents influence their children to become aggressive.

Let's practice these concepts in an official LSAT practice question. In the following Logical Reasoning question, there are three components: a passage, a question, and a set of answer choices. Read the question first. The question asks you to cast doubt on (or "weaken") the author's hypothesis. Next, read the passage, determine the author's hypothesis, and think about what would weaken it.

★ **LSAT EXAM QUESTION**

1.2.12.

A recent study found that snoring, though uncommon in either group, is more common among smokers than among nonsmokers. On the basis of this evidence, the author hypothesized that smoking by itself can induce snoring.

3. Which one of the following, if true, casts the most doubt on the author's hypothesis?

    A) Stress induces both snoring and smoking in certain individuals.

    B) Obesity induces many individuals to smoke.

C) Most snorers do not smoke.

D) Most smokers do not snore.

E) Both smoking and snoring cause throat problems.

Argument by Analogy, Example, or Illustration

An **argument by analogy** exists where you attempt to prove your conclusion by appealing to logic in a similar argument. Let's say you are trying to get a parking ticket dismissed:

> **Premise**: I got a parking ticket in front of my own house in broad daylight.
>
> **Premise**: I know I was blocking the driveway, but it was my driveway.
>
> **Premise**: Last week, Mr. Smith got a ticket for blocking the driveway in front of his own house, and he got his ticket dismissed.
>
> **Conclusion**: I should get my ticket dismissed also.

Here, you are arguing that the same reasoning that applied to Mr. Smith should apply to you as well. This style of reasoning will be one of the major components of your law school written work, so it is to your benefit to understand analogies.

Note that this is an inductive argument, which means that the conclusion does not follow with 100 percent certainty from the premises. It is certainly possible to add additional premises to the argument that would either strengthen or weaken the conclusion. For example, what if Mr. Smith were only blocking six inches of his driveway, while the author here blocked his entire driveway? Or what if Mr. Smith lived by himself, while the author here lived with others and prevented them from using the driveway? If these distinctions were true, then the argument would become weaker.

Examples and **illustrations** are different from analogies. An example or illustration is a specific instance of a broad or general statement. For example:

> **Premise**: It is unfair to prevent people from using their own property according to their wishes.
>
> **Example**: For example, it would be unfair to prevent someone from destroying artwork that they own entirely.
>
> **Conclusion**: Therefore, we should be lenient when drafting our state's property laws to allow people to use and destroy property according to their wishes.

Advocacy

Many LSAT arguments advocate a recommendation: they conclude with a statement about what someone should do in a given situation. These "should" statements are also called normative statements. A fundamental principle of logic is that, in order to prove a normative conclusion, you must have a normative premise. Consider the following argument:

Premise: Antonio, the bus driver, was going thirty-five miles per hour over the speed limit.

Premise: Antonio was also talking on his phone and trying to eat a cheeseburger.

Premise: Clearly, Antonio caused the accident.

Conclusion: Therefore, the bus company should sanction Antonio.

Now, you might be saying to yourself, "Sounds fine to me." It is true; this is not a bad argument. The problem is that we cannot conclude that the bus company should sanction Antonio without some kind of premise that defines when sanctions are appropriate. We need another premise—something like "The bus company should sanction drivers who recklessly cause accidents."

If we add this as a premise and then read our other premises (telling us that Antonio was a driver who recklessly caused an accident), *then* we can draw our conclusion with certainty.

Again, consider this argument:

Premise: Proposition 24 would cut texting while driving in half by raising the fine to $1,000.

Premise: If we cut the incidence of texting while driving in half, there would likely be five hundred fewer accidents each year.

Conclusion: Therefore, we should support Proposition 24.

What's missing here? A statement like "We should support propositions that are likely to reduce the number of accidents." If we add this "should" statement to our premises, then our conclusion is logical.

If a course of action is possible, does that mean you should do it? Even if the action has good consequences, does that necessarily mean you have an obligation to take it? Eating broccoli, creating jobs for unemployed individuals, and providing subsidized education to the poor may all be courses of action that are possible and good, but just because you *could* do something does not automatically mean that you *should*.

In your day-to-day life, you have various normative principles that tell you which courses of action you personally should do. Sometimes, a possible course of action might have significant costs or disadvantages; for example, what if Proposition 24 (discussed earlier) costs $100 million to implement and enforce. Is it still worth it? Whether it is or not is a subjective value judgment, and that is why we need to have a "should" premise in any argument in which we are trying to justify a "should" conclusion.

ARGUMENTS THAT RULE OUT ALTERNATIVES

Frequently, LSAT arguments operate by eliminating alternatives. For example, if there are three possible courses of action, an author might provide evidence that refutes two of the courses of action in order to conclude that the third is advisable. For example:

> The only ways we can maintain our market share are to develop a new
> product, to create a new marketing campaign, or to lower our prices.
> Unfortunately, lowering our prices is unrealistic, because we could
> not remain profitable. Furthermore, the costs involved in developing
> a new product are prohibitive, given our current lack of cash flow.
> Accordingly, we should start a new marketing campaign immediately.

This argument advocates one of three possible solutions, and it arrives at
its conclusion by ruling out the other two alternatives. Keep this pattern of
reasoning in mind on Method of Reasoning questions.

Predictions

Many LSAT arguments operate by making a **prediction**:

> Speeding tickets in Mason County are now so costly that no one
> saves enough money by speeding to justify paying the fine. Therefore,
> since people prefer to save money when they can, drivers will no
> longer speed in Mason County.

Notice the difference between this prediction and the earlier advocacy
examples. There are no normative statements here, nothing about whether
someone should or should not speed. This is an objective prediction about what
is likely to happen, given the premises about the cost of speeding. When you
see a prediction like this, you should consider whether the prediction is likely to
come true, based on the premises. If the prediction is likely to come true based
only on the premises stated, then the argument is strong; if the prediction is
unlikely, then the argument is weak.

Usually, these kinds of arguments do not address every possible factor that
may bear on the predicted outcome. That is, there are unknowns that impact
whether the conclusion is likely or unlikely. The author making the argument
must assume that these unknowns are in the author's favor. You can *strengthen*
a prediction by showing that these unknown factors are true, or *weaken* a prediction by showing that these unknown factors are false. For example, here is a
weaken question, based on the preceding argument:

PRACTICE QUESTION

4. Speeding tickets in Mason County are now so costly that no one saves enough
   money by speeding to justify paying the fine. Therefore, since people prefer to
   save money when they can, drivers will no longer speed in Mason County.

   Which of the following answers would weaken the argument above?

   A) People care about long-term savings as much as they care about short-
   term savings.

   B) People abide by the law only when it makes sense for them to do so.

   C) People generally underestimate the risk of being stopped for speeding.

   D) People treat speeding tickets as day-to-day expenses.

   E) People derive pleasure from speeding when police are not present.

Likelihood

Note that the word *probably* means "likely." Consider this argument: "The Tigers have the best players and the best coach, so they are probably going to win the series."

However, consider the difference between likelihood and certainty: "The Bears are the most likely team to win the playoffs. Thus, the Bears are almost certain to win."

What if there were nineteen teams in the playoffs? The Bears might have a 10 percent chance of winning, and each of the other teams might have a 5 percent chance of winning. The Bears would be the most likely to win, but with a 10 percent chance of winning, this does not support the conclusion that they will almost certainly win. Such a conclusion would require a much greater likelihood of winning than 10 percent.

Principles and Applications

What is a principle? A principle is a general rule that could apply to more than one situation. We use principles to guide our decisions, and we apply principles to situations in order to make judgments about those situations. Here are some categories of principles, with examples of each kind:

1. Moral Principles
   o An act is good if it is intended to benefit another individual and succeeds in benefiting that individual. (IB + SB → G)
   o An act is wrong only if it harms another individual. (W → H)
   o It is wrong to destroy another individual's property without permission. (WP → WD)

2. Duties and Obligations (not necessarily moral in nature)
   o Lawyers have a duty to put their clients' interests above their own.
   o People in positions of power should not exploit their influence.
   o Everyone who earns income must pay taxes.

3. General Tendencies
   o Rugby players tend to weigh more than baseball players.
   o On average, organic tomatoes are half the size of common tomatoes.
   o Slightly overweight people are generally healthier than very underweight people.

Applications

So how are principles actually used? Well, let's take our set of moral principles (above) and apply them to this scenario: "Marcia wanted to do a favor for her neighbor, David, so she shoveled the snow off of his driveway."

HELPFUL HINT

Remember to read these principles as "if...then" statements:

1. If there is intended benefit and actual benefit, then the act is good.

2. If the act is wrong, then it harmed another.

3. If the act destroys another's property and was done without permission, then it is wrong.

Based on our first principle and this scenario, what can we conclude? Marcia intended to benefit David, and Marcia succeeded in benefiting David. Therefore, Marcia's act was good.

What if we had this scenario: "Allison intentionally stepped on Christopher's foot, harming him severely."

Based on our principles and this scenario, what can we conclude? If you answered, "Nothing," then you are exactly right.

Our first principle provides that *if* there is intended benefit and actual benefit, then the act is good. Here, we do not have intended or actual benefit, so the principle cannot be used to prove anything. We move on.

Our second principle says that if an act is wrong, it must harm another individual. Another way of saying this is if an act does not harm another individual, then it is not wrong. Note that this principle can *never* be used to argue that an act is wrong. If we know that someone did not harm another, then we know that an act is not wrong, but we have no basis whatsoever for concluding that an act is wrong. Just because an act harms another individual does not mean it is wrong; that would invoke a mistaken reversal. The only valid arguments you can make using the second principle are as follows:

> An act is wrong only if it harms another individual. (W → H)
>
> Ben's act was wrong. (W)
>
> Therefore, Ben's act harmed someone else. (W → H)
>
> *or*
>
> An act is wrong only if it harms another individual. Ben's act did not harm anyone else.
>
> Therefore, Ben's act was not wrong.

In shorthand, our principle is "wrong → harm." The only things this principle can prove are "harm" (given the premise "wrong"), or "~wrong" (given the premise "~harm").

If you wanted to prove that an act was wrong, you would need a principle that you could write out as "[set of conditions] → wrong." For example, you might create the principle "It is wrong to injure another individual's body parts intentionally." Then, given our scenario with Allison, we would be able to conclude logically that Allison's act of intentionally stepping on Christopher's foot was wrong.

LOGICAL REASONING TIP

On many Logical Reasoning questions, you will be asked to add principles into arguments to "justify" the conclusion (that is, to make the conclusion 100 percent certain, based on the premises and your new principle). Look carefully at the conclusion. If the conclusion says, "We should save the bald eagle," what do you need to look for? A premise that tells you what you *should* save, not a premise that tells you what you *should not* save.

Try adding in a principle to justify this argument:

> Our borders are vulnerable to enemy attack, so we should deploy additional troops. (V → D)

You do not want an answer that says "When borders are secure, we should not deploy additional troops." You want an answer that says "When borders are not secure, we should deploy additional troops" (NS → D). That is the sort of principle that will justify the conclusion in the argument.

Answer Key

Questions marked with a star are official LSAT questions provided by the LSAC.

1. These statements are variants of "If B, then I": B, D, E, K, L, M, O, P, Q, R, and U.

    These statements are variants of "If I, then B": A, C, F, G, H, J, N, S, T, V, W, and X.

2. A) If you complete law school, then you have read a lot.

    B) If Mark became a Supreme Court clerk, then he developed better interviewing skills.

    C) If Griswold was elected, then he must have changed his rhetoric.

    D) If the tide has not come in, then she sells seashells on the seashore.

    E) If it is a whale, then it is a mammal.

    F) If it is a whale, then it is a mammal.

    G) If Slovakia refrains from invading Poland, then there was rapid economic improvement.

    H) If meteors killed the dinosaurs, then debris is fatal.

    I) If it is available for five dollars from Jimmy John's, then it is a ham and cheese sandwich. (Note: "If it is a five dollars sandwich from Jimmy John's, then it is ham and cheese" is incorrect. This would allow other food items besides sandwiches to be available for five dollars, which is inconsistent with the condition expressed.)

    J) If my cell phone rings, then I forgot to turn it on silent.

    K) If Lindsey suffers from acid reflux, then she has eaten too many hot peppers.

★ 3. Notice the leap from the premises to the conclusion. The premises support a correlation between smoking and snoring. The conclusion argues that smoking causes snoring. However, as we saw earlier, there are alternative possibilities that this argument has failed to eliminate.

    What are all of the possibilities?

    1. It is possible that smoking really does cause snoring.

    2. It is possible that snoring might cause people to smoke.

    3. Alternatively, a third factor might cause both snoring and smoking.

    4. Finally, smoking and snoring might be merely coincidental.

    Since the author's hypothesis depends upon the truth of the first possibility, we can weaken his argument by having one of the other possibilities be true instead.

    Let's find an answer:

A) is correct. This choice tells us that stress (an outside factor) causes both snoring and smoking. This is exactly what we are looking for. If this is true (and the question told you to assume that it is), then snoring does not cause smoking; stress does. This is a great weakener, because it provides an alternative cause of smoking while also explaining why there is a correlation between smoking and snoring. If you ruled out answer A) because the passage did not talk about stress, then you did not look at the question the right way. This question specifically asks you to consider which answer, if true, would weaken the hypothesis. Even if the answer said, "Phases of the moon induce both snoring and smoking," it would still have been correct. See Weaken Questions in Chapter 3, "Logical Reasoning Questions."

B) is incorrect. This choice tells us about an alternative cause of smoking—obesity—but that does not help us in this argument because our conclusion concerns what causes snoring.

C) is incorrect. This choice does not weaken the argument, because it is fully consistent with snoring being the cause of smoking. Knowing which portion of each group does or does not snore has no bearing on whether smoking causes snoring.

D) is incorrect. This choice does not weaken the argument, because the author has already said that snoring is not common among smokers, implying that most smokers do not snore. Choice D) is fully consistent with this premise.

E) is incorrect. While choice E) may look similar to answer A), E) tells us that smoking and snoring cause *something else*. It does not present a common factor that causes them. Knowing that smoking and snoring also cause other phenomena does not help to explain what causes snoring.

4. **C) is correct.** This choice weakens the argument by telling us that people do not know when they stand to be pulled over. Thus, even though speeding tickets cost more than people will save by speeding, people may continue to speed because they think they will get away with it.

Answer choice D) is a distractor. The passage told us that people prefer to save money when they can, so it does not matter how people account for their speeding tickets. Whether they are day-to-day expenses or special expenses, people still want to avoid them when it is worthwhile to do so.

2 | Flawed Patterns of Reasoning

Common Fallacies on the LSAT

Now that we have seen some of the ways in which arguments work, let's run through some of the common ways in which arguments go wrong.

The LSAT evaluates your ability to analyze the logical soundness of an argument. In Logical Reasoning, and occasionally in Reading Comprehension questions, the LSAT will ask readers to identify what is wrong with an argument. Before reviewing the answer choices, you must be able to spot logical errors (fallacies or flaws) to understand why an argument is flawed.

In Analytical Reasoning (Logic Games), certain incorrect answers will appear correct if you have mistakenly committed a fallacy (such as a mistaken reversal) while attempting to solve the problem. Mastering the fallacies discussed in this chapter will help you to avoid committing them yourself and will enable you to spot them on the test.

The LSAT commonly tests twenty-four fallacies. Nineteen are fallacies of inductive reasoning, as shown in Table 2.1.

TABLE 2.1. The Nineteen Fallacies of Inductive Reasoning: Informal Logic	
Fallacies of relevance	• appeal to emotion (*ad populum*) • argument against the person (*ad hominem*) • false analogy • red herring • straw man • absolute properties versus relative properties; numbers and proportions • missing the point (*non sequitur*)
Fallacies of strength	• argument from ignorance • appeal to inappropriate authority • false cause • hasty generalization

continued on next page

TABLE 2.1. The Nineteen Fallacies of Inductive Reasoning: Informal Logic (continued)	
Fallacies of presumption	• accident; "can" versus "will" • unjustified assumption • circular reasoning • false dilemma • starting point fallacy
Fallacies of ambiguity	• equivocation • composition • division

The other five are fallacies of deductive reasoning (formal logic):

1. mistaken reversal

2. mistaken negation

3. either-or fallacy

4. undistributed middle

5. contradiction

To spot fallacies quickly and precisely, you should have a solid understanding of these twenty-four fallacies. Some courses and materials contain a seemingly endless list of fallacies (as many as one hundred). Resist the urge to create new categories; the fallacies that you will encounter on the LSAT will fall into the categories given here.

When you see a fallacy that appears to be a new type, stop and consider the twenty-four fallacies and where that fallacy belongs. If you cannot place the fallacy as a variation on one of the twenty-four, at least place it in one of the five broad categories: relevance, strength, presumption, ambiguity, or formal logic.

As you work through Argument Flaw Logical Reasoning questions, spend time reviewing those that you miss to make sure you understand exactly which fallacy the argument is committing.

Learning twenty-four fallacies is a manageable task, especially if you learn them in groups and develop working definitions and examples of each type.

Each of the following twenty-four entries contains:

- the common name of the fallacy.

- an explanation of the fallacy.

- the definition of the fallacy, worded to reflect the wording of the answer choices you will see on Argument Flaw Logical Reasoning questions.

- an example of the fallacy from real life.

- an example of the fallacy from an actual LSAT Logical Reasoning question.

 **DID YOU KNOW?**

Readers who commit the fallacies of deductive reasoning are especially vulnerable in Analytical Reasoning questions.

Expect to encounter these fallacies in almost every type of Logical Reasoning question on the test, as well as in some Reading Comprehension passages. Be careful not to commit these fallacies yourself; you may find yourself attracted to incorrect answer choices.

Fallacies of Relevance

In **fallacies of relevance**, an author either uses an irrelevant premise in an argument or makes the wrong conclusion altogether.

The following are fallacies of relevance using **irrelevant premises**:

- **appeal to emotion** *(ad populum)*: persuasion by emotional rather than by intellectual means

- **argument against the person** *(ad hominem)*: arguing against another's argument by attacking that person's character or conduct

- **false analogy**: supporting a conclusion by means of an apparent analogy without justifying the proposition that the two arguments are actually worthy of comparison

- **red herring** *(a broad category that includes appeal to emotion, argument against the person, and false analogy)*: offering a deliberately misleading premise

The following are fallacies of relevance using **mistaken conclusions**:

- **straw man**: distorting an opponent's argument to make it easier to defeat

- **absolute properties versus relative properties** *(numbers and proportions)*: using a relative property (or percentage) as a premise and an absolute property (or number) as a conclusion

- **missing the point** *(non sequitur)* **(a broad category that includes straw man and numbers and propositions)**: drawing an irrelevant, mistaken, or overbroad conclusion; jumping to conclusions

Appeal to Emotion

Ordinarily, arguments work by appealing to reason. Given a set of facts, the reader's reasoning leads the reader to agree with the author's conclusion. Sometimes, however, authors will appeal to the reader's emotions (conscience, fear, or sense of pity) to get the reader to agree with a point. **Appeals to emotion** may include emotionally charged language.

Sample LSAT answer choices that reflect this fallacy include statements

- that seek to persuade by emotional rather than by intellectual means.

- in which the author appeals to conscience rather than reason.

- that use emotive language in labeling the proposals.

- that use hyperbolic, inflammatory language that obscures the issue at hand.

- that appeal to a person's emotions rather than to her reason.

> **Example**: Advertisements and patriotism are common sources of emotional appeals:
>
> 1. Everyone in the know reads the *Wall Street Journal*. Subscribe today!
>
> 2. Ronald fought tooth and nail for our country's independence. He poured his sweat and blood out for our freedom. How could any worthy citizen now turn his back on such a gallant candidate for office as Ronald?

1. This example appeals to the conscience of the reader by making the reader feel left out; however, no rational basis is provided for subscribing. This is also called the **bandwagon effect**.

2. This use of patriotism appeals to the audience's emotions; no rational basis is provided to support Ronald's candidacy for office.

★ **LSAT EXAM QUESTION**

26.1.1

Insurance that was to become effective at 9:00 a.m. on a certain date was taken out on the life of a flight attendant. He died on that date at 10:00 a.m. local time, which was two hours before 9:00 a.m. in the time zone where the policy had been purchased. The insurance company contended that the policy had not become effective; a representative of the flight attendant's beneficiary, his mother, countered by arguing that the policy amount should be paid because the attendant had been his mother's sole support, and she was ill.

1. The representative's argument is flawed as a counter to the insurance company's contention because

   A) the conclusion is no more than a paraphrase of the evidence offered in support of it.

   B) it appeals to the emotion of pity rather than addressing the issue being raised.

   C) it makes an unwarranted distinction between family obligations and business obligations.

   D) it substitutes an attack on a person for the giving of reasons.

   E) a cause and its effect are mistaken for each other.

Argument Against the Person (*ad hominem*)

If your argument is directed against your opponents' conclusion, it is a fallacy to use a premise that attacks your opponents themselves. That is, you should always argue against the opposing argument, not against the source of the opposing argument.

It is an **attack against the person** to use a premise about a person's character or conduct to support a conclusion about that person's argument. This is a fallacy because the person's character is usually unrelated to the person's argument. A premise that concerns the person's character is irrelevant to your conclusion.

HELPFUL HINT

The following would NOT be an attack on the person: "Dr. Ziegler is not organized and fails to keep complete records on his patient. Therefore, Dr. Ziegler is not a responsible physician." This is not a fallacy because the conclusion is about the doctor. Some LSAT questions trap you into identifying an argument like this as an ad hominem argument. However, when the argument's premises AND conclusion are about a person, even where the argument overtly attacks that person, it is not a fallacy. The fallacy occurs when the conclusion is about the person's argument (or book, or position), and the premise is about the person himself. Facts about a person are irrelevant to a conclusion about a person's argument.

Sample LSAT answer choices that reflect this fallacy include:

- avoids the issue by focusing on supporters of the proposal

- attacking the opponents' motives instead of their argument

- questioning the motives of one side rather than offering reasons for the conclusion defended

- rejecting the conclusion of an argument on the basis of a claim about the motives of those advancing the argument

- calls into question the truthfulness of the opponent rather than addressing the point at issue

- dismisses the proposals because of their source rather than because of their substance

- draws conclusions about the merit of a position and about the content of that position from evidence about the position's source

Example: Imagine Tom wrote a book, and someone comes along and says, "Don't read that book. It can't be any good. Tom's the most selfish guy I know." This person is trying to argue that the book is not worth reading, but his premise is that the book's author is selfish. This premise is irrelevant because it attacks the book's author rather than the book itself.

★ LSAT EXAM QUESTION

4.1.16.

The current proposal to give college students a broader choice in planning their own courses of study should be abandoned. The students who are supporting the proposal will never be satisfied, no matter what requirements are established. Some of these students have reached their third year without declaring a major. One first-year student has failed to complete four required courses. Several others have indicated a serious indifference to grades and intellectual achievement.

2. A flaw in the argument is that it does which one of the following?

   A) avoids the issue by focusing on supporters of the proposal

   B) argues circularly by assuming the conclusion is true in stating the premises

   C) fails to define the critical term *satisfied*

   D) distorts the proposal advocated by opponents

   E) uses the term *students* equivocally

False Analogy

A common pattern of reasoning is to make an argument by analogy. However, every analogy is not necessarily a good analogy. Just because two arguments are similar in one way does not mean they are similar in every other important way. A **false analogy** is when premises do not support a comparison between the primary argument and the analogous argument.

A sample LSAT answer choice that reflects this fallacy treats two kinds of things that differ in important respects as though they do not differ.

> **Example**: "John was overweight. He started eating spinach and subsequently lost twenty pounds. Therefore, if Jerry, who is also overweight, starts eating spinach, he will lose twenty pounds." John's weight loss is an analogous situation to Jerry's situation because the two were both overweight, but we do not know anything else about John and Jerry. Perhaps John was also exercising while he ate the spinach. Or perhaps Jerry has a medical condition that will prevent him from losing twenty pounds. Do not assume that whatever applies to John must also apply to Jerry. When you are being asked to identify a fallacy, you should note that the argument fails to consider the possibility that the two situations are not comparable.

★ LSAT EXAM QUESTION

3.1.5.

Observatory director: "Some say that funding the mega-telescope will benefit only the astronomers who will work with it. This dangerous point of view, applied to the work of Maxwell, Newton, or Einstein, would have stifled their research and deprived the world of beneficial applications, such as the development of radio, which followed from that research."

3. If the preceding statements are put forward as an argument in favor of development of the mega-telescope, which one of the following is the strongest criticism of this argument?

   A) It appeals to the authority of experts who cannot have known all the issues involved in construction of the mega-telescope.

   B) It does not identify those opposed to development of the mega-telescope.

   C) It launches a personal attack on opponents of the mega-telescope by accusing them of having a dangerous point of view.

   D) It does not distinguish between the economic and the intellectual senses of "benefit."

   E) It does not show that the proposed mega-telescope research is worthy of comparison with that of eminent scientists in its potential for applications.

Red Herring

A **red herring** is any irrelevant premise offered along the way to a conclusion. Ad hominem attacks and appeals to emotion fall into this category as well, because they are irrelevant premises. Any deliberately misleading premise falls into this broad category; consider the red herring as a sort of catchall for irrelevant information that masquerades as support for an argument.

Sample LSAT answer choices that reflect this fallacy include:

- attempts to justify a position by appeal to an irrelevant consideration

- basing its conclusion on evidence that is almost entirely irrelevant to the point at hand
- The author citing irrelevant data

> **Example**: "Over the past ten years, people in Springfield have increasingly reported a belief that crime is out of control. Clearly, Springfield needs to hire more police officers." Here, the red herring is presenting the people's belief as evidence, instead of presenting actual crime statistics. Popular opinion is not the same as factual evidence, so this is a deliberately misleading premise.
>
> **Example**: "Labrador Bus Lines is clearly the best choice for a safe trip, because it consistently files the most complete annual safety reports of any transportation provider in the country." The bus company may file complete reports, but that does not necessarily mean that it has a record of safety. Labrador's administrative responsibility is a red herring; knowing that the company actually has a solid safety record would be a relevant premise.

★ LSAT EXAM QUESTION

7.1.17.

Office manager: "I will not order recycled paper for this office.
Our letters to clients must make a good impression, so we cannot print them on inferior paper."

Stationary supplier: "Recycled paper is not necessarily inferior. In fact, from the beginning, the finest paper has been made of recycled material. It was only in the 1850s that paper began to be made from wood fiber, and then only because there were no longer enough rags to meet the demand for paper."

4. In which one of the following ways does the stationer's response fail to address the office manager's objection to recycled paper?

   A) It does not recognize that the office manager's prejudice against recycled paper stems from ignorance.

   B) It uses irrelevant facts to justify a claim about the quality of the disputed product.

   C) It assumes that the office manager is concerned about environmental issues.

   D) It presupposes that the office manager understands the basic technology of paper manufacturing.

   E) It ignores the office manager's legitimate concern about quality.

Straw Man

Making a **straw man** argument is like putting words in somebody's mouth. In a straw man, one person makes a standard argument. Then another person distorts the first person's argument into something more extreme and easier to defeat than it actuality was. The second person turns the original argument into a hollow "straw man" version, which can be easily picked apart. This is a fallacy because the second person has not actually defeated the original argument; they have only defeated the straw man version of the argument.

Sample LSAT answer choices that reflect this fallacy include:

- misrepresents the position against which it is directed
- distorts the proposal advocated by opponents
- gives a distorted version of one person's proposals and then attacks this distorted version
- The position being argued against is redefined unfairly in order to make it an easier target.

> **Example**: Person 1: "Modest consumption of red wine protects against artery damage and increases the level of 'good' cholesterol in the blood. Therefore, modest consumption of red wine can be good for the heart."
>
> Person 2: "What you're saying is that I should drink more alcohol in order to be healthier. But surely that's not right! People suffer from liver disease and all kinds of negative effects because of heavy alcohol consumption."

The fallacy occurs when Person 2 says, "What you're saying is…" but then *distorts* what Person 1 is actually saying. Person 1 said that modest wine consumption could be good for the heart. Person 2 has distorted this statement, changing "modest wine consumption" to "more alcohol," and changing "good for the heart" to "healthier." Then, Person 2 defeats the argument that drinking more alcohol would make him healthier. This is the wrong conclusion, however, because Person 2 should have been arguing the real issue: whether modest wine consumption can be good for the heart.

★ LSAT EXAM QUESTION

7.2.9.

Student representative: "Our university, in expelling a student who verbally harassed his roommate, has erred by penalizing the student for doing what he surely has a right to do: speak his mind!"

Dean of students: "But what you're saying is that our university should endorse verbal harassment. Yet surely if we did that, we would threaten the free flow of ideas that is the essence of university life."

5. Which one of the following is a questionable technique that the dean of students uses in attempting to refute the student representative?

    A) challenging the student representative's knowledge of the process by which the student was expelled

    B) invoking a fallacious distinction between speech and other sorts of behavior

    C) misdescribing the student representative's position, thereby making it easier to challenge

    D) questioning the motives of the student representative rather than offering reasons for the conclusion defended

E) relying on a position of power to silence the opponent's viewpoint with a threat

Absolute Versus Relative; Numbers Versus Proportions

Explanation: Words like *healthy*, *easy*, and *wise* are absolute properties when compared with words like *healthier*, *easier*, and *wiser* (relative properties). You will encounter bad arguments where the premises contain a relative property, and the conclusion contains an absolute property (e.g., "LSAT Reading Comprehension is less difficult than GRE verbal; therefore, the LSAT is easy").

You will also encounter bad arguments where the premises discuss absolute numbers, but the conclusion sneakily switches the matter under discussion to a proportion, or vice versa.

Sample LSAT answer choices that reflect this fallacy include:

- It takes no account of the relative frequency of an absolute property.
- It bases a comparison on percentages rather than on absolute numbers.
- The argument mistakes a merely relative property for one that is absolute.

Example: Ten percent of left-handed people play the piano, and 40 percent of right-handed people play the piano. Therefore, most piano players must be right-handed.

At first glance, this might look like a valid argument, but it makes a wrong conclusion. The problem here is that the proportions in our premises tell us what percentage of left-handed people and right-handed people play the piano, but our conclusion switches to a percentage of piano players. Based on the premises, we have no way of knowing how many piano players are left-handed and how many piano players are right-handed, so we cannot draw this conclusion.

After all, it may be the case that there are one million left-handed people and only one hundred right-handed people. In such a case, even if 40 percent of right-handed people play the piano, the argument's conclusion would be false, because most piano players would be left-handed.

Finally, remember not to bring in outside information like "most people are right-handed." That is the kind of error that will keep you from seeing the fallacy at all.

★ LSAT EXAM QUESTION

12.1.14.

Morris High School has introduced a policy designed to improve the working conditions of its new teachers. As a result of this policy, only one quarter of all part-time teachers quit during their first year. However, a third of all full-time teachers quit during their first year. Thus, more full-time than part-time teachers at Morris quit during their first year.

6. The argument's reasoning is questionable because the argument fails to rule out the possibility that

A) before the new policy was instituted, more part-time than full-time teachers at Morris High School used to quit during their first year.

B) before the new policy was instituted, the same number of full-time teachers as part-time teachers at Morris High School used to quit during their first year.

C) Morris High School employs more new full-time teachers than part-time teachers.

D) Morris High School employs more new part-time teachers than new full-time teachers.

E) Morris High School employs the same number of new part-time and full-time teachers.

Missing the Point

Missing the point is the fallacy of jumping to conclusions. When your premises appear to lead you to a certain conclusion, but you end up concluding something else altogether (or something more extreme than would follow logically), you miss the point. Missing the point involves making an irrelevant, mistaken, or overbroad conclusion.

Sample LSAT answer choices that reflect this fallacy include:

- draws a conclusion that is broader in scope than is warranted by the evidence advanced

- ignoring available, potentially useful counterevidence

- offering as an adequate defense of a practice an observation that discredits only one of several possible alternatives to that practice

- fails to give any reason for the judgment it reaches

- argues against a point that is not one that she was making

> **Example**: A promising new restaurant has just opened on Fourth Street. Unless it markets itself better, however, it will not attract much of a dinner crowd. Therefore, the restaurant's success depends on improving its marketing campaign.

The premises support the idea that the restaurant could increase its patronage with better marketing, but the conclusion goes too far, arguing that success depends on better marketing. This argument has missed the point.

★ LSAT EXAM QUESTION

9.1.5.

Advertisement: "Northwoods Maple Syrup, made the old-fashioned way, is simply tops for taste. And here is the proof: in a recent market survey, seven out of every ten shoppers who expressed a preference said that Northwoods was the only maple syrup for them, no ifs, ands, or buts."

7. Of the following, which one is the strongest reason why the advertisement is potentially misleading?

A) The proportion of shoppers expressing no preference might have been very small.

B) Other brands of maple syrup might also be made the old-fashioned way.

C) No market survey covers more than a sizable minority of the total population of consumers.

D) The preference for the Northwoods brand might be based on a factor such as an exceptionally low price.

E) Shoppers who buy syrup might buy only maple syrup.

Fallacies of Strength

In **fallacies of strength**, an author might have relevant premises, but the premises are too weak to support the conclusion.

The following are fallacies of strength:

- **argument from ignorance**: concluding that something is true because it has not been proven false, or vice versa

- **appeal to inappropriate authority**: citing an expert as support for an argument in a field beyond the expert's expertise

- **false cause**: confusing correlation with causation, or switching a cause and an effect

- **hasty generalization**: drawing a broad conclusion on the basis of a small or unfair sample

Argument from Ignorance

Just because something has not been proven true does not mean it is necessarily false. Likewise, just because something has not been proven false does not mean it is necessarily true. An argument that attempts to use either of these lines of reasoning is an **argument from ignorance**. To remember this fallacy, consider the adage "Absence of evidence is not evidence of absence."

Sample LSAT answer choices that reflect this fallacy include:

- confuses an absence of evidence for a hypothesis with the existence of evidence against the hypothesis

- takes the failure of a given argument to establish its conclusion as the basis for claiming that the view expressed by that conclusion is false

- takes lack of evidence for the existence of a state of affairs as evidence that there can be no such state of affairs

> **Example**: Both of the following arguments are arguments from ignorance:
>
> You have no evidence to prove there is a God. Therefore, God does not exist. You have no evidence to prove there is not a God, so God does exist.

★ LSAT EXAM QUESTION

11.2.3.

A group of scientists, who have done research on the health effects of food irradiation, have discovered no evidence challenging its safety. Supporters of food irradiation have cited this research as certain proof that food irradiation is a safe practice.

8. A flaw in the supporters' reasoning is that they

A) assume that the scientists doing the research set out to prove that food irradiation is an unsafe practice.

B) are motivated by a biased interest in proving the practice to be safe.

C) overlook the possibility that objections about safety are not the only possible objections to the practice.

D) neglect to provide detailed information about the evidence used to support the conclusion.

E) use the lack of evidence contradicting a claim as conclusive evidence for that claim.

Appeal to Inappropriate Authority

Experts are useful, but only in their fields of expertise. An **appeal to inappropriate authority** is citing an expert as support for an argument in a field beyond the expert's expertise. Many advertisements commit this fallacy when they use a celebrity to endorse a product that the celebrity may know nothing about.

Sample LSAT answer choices that reflect this fallacy include:

- makes an illegitimate appeal to the authority of an expert
- makes an irrelevant appeal to an authority

> **Example**: "People say that businesses are moving out of Smithtown at an increasing rate. But Jane, a distinguished mathematician, says this is not the case. So clearly, people are mistaken." The fallacy here is appealing to a mathematician's opinion in an argument about commerce.

★ LSAT EXAM QUESTION

6.1.5.

The museum's night security guard maintains that the thieves who stole the portrait did not enter the museum from any point at or above ground level. Therefore, the thieves must have gained access to the museum from below ground level.

(Unlike most of the other questions in this chapter, this question asks you to find an answer that has an argument committing the same fallacy as the argument in the preceding passage.)

9. The flawed pattern of reasoning in the preceding argument is most similar to which one of the following?

A) The rules stipulate the participants in the contest be judged on both form and accuracy. The eventual winner was judged highest in neither category, so there must be a third criterion that judges were free to invoke.

B) The store's competitors claim that the store, in selling off the shirts at those prices, neither made any profit nor broke even. Consequently, the store's customers must have been able to buy shirts at less than the store's cost.

C) If the census is to be believed, the percentage of men who are married is higher than the percentage of women who are married. Thus, the census must show a higher number of men than of women overall.

D) The product label establishes that this insecticide is safe for both humans and pets. Therefore, the insecticide must also be safe for wild mammals such as deer and rabbits.

E) As had generally been expected, not all questionnaires were sent in by the official deadline. It follows that plans must have been made for the processing of questionnaires received late.

False Cause

A mere correlation between two events does not prove causation. **False cause**—switching cause for effect, or confusing correlation for causation—is a common fallacy on the LSAT. Any time you see "cause" in a conclusion (or any of its synonyms), look for one of these mistakes: confusing a correlation for causation, confusing a temporal relationship (A happened before B) for causation (A caused B), or confusing a cause for an effect.

Sample LSAT answer choices that reflect this fallacy include:

- assumes a causal relationship where only a correlation has been indicated
- mistakes the observation that one thing happens after another for proof that the second thing is the result of the first
- confusing the coincidence of two events with a causal relation between the two
- mistaking an effect for a cause
- explaining one event as being caused by another event, even though both events must have actually been caused by some third, unidentified event

> **Example:** "Two years ago, I started buying my parts from Vic's. Now, all my customers have left. Clearly, Vic's parts have cost me my livelihood." Just because customers left following the author's decision to buy parts from Vic's does not mean that Vic's parts caused the customers to leave.

★ LSAT EXAM QUESTION

14.2.20.

Monroe, despite his generally poor appetite, thoroughly enjoyed the three meals he ate at the Tip Top Restaurant, but unfortunately, after each meal he became ill. The first time he ate an extra-large sausage pizza with a side order of hot peppers, the second time he took full advantage of the All-You-Can-Eat Fried Shrimp and

Hot Peppers special, and the third time he had two of Tip Top's giant meatball sandwiches with hot peppers. Since the only food all three meals had in common was the hot peppers, Monroe concludes that it is solely due to Tip Top's hot peppers that he became ill.

10. Monroe's reasoning is most vulnerable to which one of the following criticisms?

   A) He draws his conclusion based on too few meals with hot peppers consumed at Tip Top.

   B) He posits a causal relationship without ascertaining that the presumed cause preceded the presumed effect.

   C) He allows his desire to continue dining at Tip Top to bias his conclusion.

   D) He fails to establish that everyone who ate Tip Top's hot peppers became ill.

   E) He overlooks the fact that at all three meals he consumed what was, for him, an unusually large quantity of food.

Hasty Generalization

Drawing a conclusion about a large group of people or events requires more than a few pieces of evidence. Drawing a broad conclusion based on one or a few instances (or an unfair sample) is a **hasty generalization**.

The term *general* as in *general principle* or *generalization* is important. If a statement applies generally, that means that the statement applies to "most" cases—that is, to more than half of potential cases. "Bob eats candy when he is very hungry" is not a general principle because it can only apply to Bob. "People tend to eat unhealthy food when they become very hungry" is a general principle because it can be applied to specific people and specific food selections.

Sample LSAT answer choices that reflect this fallacy include:

- relies on evidence drawn from a sample that there is reason to believe is unrepresentative

- generalizes from only a few instances

- a few exceptional cases as the basis for a claim about what is true in general

- generalizes on the basis of a sample consisting of atypical cases

> **Example:** "My friend Marty has eaten red meat three times a day for forty years, and his health is excellent, so surely there is nothing wrong with eating lots of red meat." This argument hastily generalizes from Marty to a generic statement about the merits of eating meat. Just because Marty can eat a large quantity of meat does not mean everyone else can.

5.1.2.

College professor: "College students do not write nearly as well as they used to. Almost all of the papers my students have done for me this year have been poorly written and ungrammatical."

11. Which one of the following is the most serious weakness in the argument made by the professor?

   A) It requires confirmation that the change in the professor's students is representative of a change among college students in general.

   B) It offers no proof to the effect that the professor is an accurate judge of writing ability.

   C) It does not take into account the possibility that the professor is a poor teacher.

   D) It fails to present contrary evidence.

   E) It fails to define its terms sufficiently.

Fallacies of Presumption

In **fallacies of presumption**, the author assumes that an important part of the argument is true without providing a logical basis for making such an assumption.

The following are fallacies of presumption:

- **accident; "can" versus "will"**: applying a general rule to an individual case without considering whether the individual may be the exception to the rule; confusing a possibility with certainty

- **unjustified assumption**: assuming a premise of an argument without justification

- **circular reasoning**: assuming the conclusion is true in order to prove the conclusion is true

- **false dilemma:** presenting two of several alternatives as though they were the only possible alternatives

- **starting point fallacy**: attempting to evaluate the effects of a change without knowing the facts as they existed before the change

Accident; "Can" Versus "Will"

Accident is the opposite of hasty generalization. Hasty generalization occurs when you use one or a few instances to justify a general conclusion. On the other hand, the fallacy of **accident** occurs when you use a general principle to justify a conclusion about a specific individual without stopping to think about why that individual might be an exception to the rule.

Sample LSAT answer choices that reflect this fallacy will:

- apply a generalization to an exceptional case.

- attribute to every member of the population the properties of the average member of the population.

> **Example:** "On average, graduating law students who secure jobs will earn $129,000 per year. Maria just graduated law school and has a full-time job lined up. So, Maria will be earning $129,000 next year." The problem here is that we have taken an average and rigidly applied it to Maria's specific situation without considering that Maria might have a higher- or lower-paying job.
>
> **Example:** "People who work fifteen or more hours a day tend to take active vacations. Marcus works sixteen hours a day, so he must prefer active vacations to lying around on the beach." The problem here is that Marcus might be an exception to the rule.

★ LSAT EXAM QUESTION

12.1.17.

On average, city bus drivers who are using the new computerized fare collection system have a much better on-time record than do drivers using the old fare collection system. Millicent Smith has the best on-time record of any bus driver in the city. Therefore, she must be using the computerized fare collection system.

Note that unlike most of the other questions in this chapter, this question asks you to find an answer in which an argument commits the same fallacy as the argument in the preceding passage.

12. Which one of the following contains flawed reasoning most similar to that contained in the preceding argument?

A) All of the city's solid waste collection vehicles acquired after 1988 have a larger capacity than any of those acquired before 1988. This vehicle has the largest capacity of any the city owns, so it must have been acquired after 1988.

B) The soccer players on the blue team are generally taller than the players on the gold team. Since Henri is a member of the blue team, he is undoubtedly taller than most of the members of the gold team.

C) This tomato is the largest of this year's crop. Since the tomatoes in the experimental plot are on average larger than those grown in the regular plots, this tomato must have been grown in the experimental plot.

D) Last week's snowstorm in Toronto was probably an average storm for the area. It was certainly heavier than any snowstorm known to have occurred in Miami, but any average snowstorm in Toronto leaves more snow than ever falls in Miami.

E) Lawn mowers powered by electricity generally require less maintenance than do lawn mowers powered by gasoline. This lawn mower is powered by gasoline, so it will probably require a lot of maintenance.

Unjustified Assumption

An **unjustified assumption** is when an argument must establish a premise in order to arrive at a conclusion, and it assumes, rather than proves, that premise.

Sample LSAT answer choices that reflect this fallacy include:

- presumes that most consumers heed the warning labels on beverage containers

- assumes that the fact of an error is proof of an intention to deceive

> **Example**: "Getting into Harvard Law School requires nothing more than an undergraduate degree, a competitive LSAT score, excellent letters of recommendation, and a solid personal statement. Cheryl has excellent recommendation letters, a very competitive LSAT score, and a bachelor's degree in chemical engineering, so she'll get into Harvard Law School." The argument never states that Cheryl had a solid personal statement, which makes its conclusion an unjustified assumption.

★ LSAT EXAM QUESTION

3.2.18.

Physicalists expect that ultimately all mental functions will be explainable in neurobiological terms. Achieving this goal requires knowledge of neurons and their basic functions, how neurons interact, and a delineation of the psychological faculties to be explained. At present, there is a substantial amount of fundamental knowledge about the basic functions of neurons, and the scope and character of such psychological capacities as visual perception and memory are well understood. Thus, as the physicalists claim, mental functions are bound to receive explanations in neurobiological terms in the near future.

13. Which one of the following indicates an error in the reasoning in the passage?

   A) The conclusion contradicts the claim of the physicalists.

   B) The passage fails to describe exactly what is currently known about neurons' basic functions.

   C) The word *neurobiological* is used as though it had the same meaning as the word *mental*.

   D) The argument does not indicate whether it would be useful to explain mental functions in neurobiological terms.

   E) The passage does not indicate that any neuron-interaction knowledge has been achieved.

Circular Reasoning (Begging the Question)

Circular reasoning occurs when the author restates the argument's conclusion as support for the conclusion. Circular reasoning is also called **begging the question**. It is usually easy to spot because it repeats the conclusion, in some form, as a premise of the argument.

Sample LSAT answer choices that reflect this fallacy include:

- The reasons given in support of the conclusion presuppose the truth of that conclusion.
- The argument is a circular argument made up of an opening claim followed by a conclusion that merely paraphrases that claim.
- It assumes what it seeks to establish.
- It presupposes that which is to be proved.
- It assumes at the outset what the argument claims to establish through reasoning.

Example: "Our cookies are healthy, and we know they're healthy because the kinds of people who buy our cookies buy healthy things. How do we know that our customers buy healthy things? Because they buy our healthy cookies." The conclusion of the argument is "Our cookies are healthy," but this is also a premise of the argument.

Example: In the movie *The Pearls of the Crown*, three thieves fight over seven valuable pearls. The thief in the middle gives two pearls to the thief on his right and two to the thief on his left. "I will keep three," he says. "How come you keep three?" says the man on his right. "Because I am the leader." "Oh. But why are you the leader?" "Because I have more pearls."

★ LSAT EXAM QUESTION

36.1.10.

Cotrell is, at best, able to write magazine articles of average quality. The most compelling pieces of evidence for this are those few of the numerous articles submitted by Cotrell that are superior, since Cotrell, who is incapable of writing an article that is better than average, must obviously have plagiarized superior ones.

14. The argument is most vulnerable to criticism on which one of the following grounds?

- **A)** It simply ignores the existence of potential counterevidence.
- **B)** It generalizes from atypical occurrences.
- **C)** It presupposes what it seeks to establish.
- **D)** It relies on the judgment of experts in a matter in which their expertise is irrelevant.
- **E)** It infers limits on ability from a few isolated lapses in performance.

False Dilemma

If you set up a situation in which there appears to be only two alternatives, but in reality there may be other options, you have created a **false dilemma**. A false dilemma may also exist where an argument discusses a group of individuals but only discusses the two extremes of a group without considering the middle of the group.

Sample LSAT answer choices that reflect this fallacy include:

- It assumes without warrant that a situation allows only two possibilities.
- It sets up a dichotomy between alternatives that are not exclusive.

> **Example**: "If we don't market our new products better, we will cease being competitive. You have my marketing plan in front of you. So, either we act on this plan, or we'll end up losing our competitiveness." This is a false dilemma because the author sets up the two apparent alternatives: follow his plan, or do not take any action at all. What if there are other marketing plans?

★ LSAT EXAM QUESTION

7.2.3.

When workers do not find their assignments challenging, they become bored and so achieve less than their abilities would allow. On the other hand, when workers find their assignments too difficult, they give up and so again achieve less than what they are capable of achieving. It is, therefore, clear that no worker's full potential will ever be realized.

15. Which one of the following is an error of reasoning contained in the argument?

  A) mistakenly equates what is actual and what is merely possible

  B) assumes without warrant that a situation allows only two possibilities

  C) relies on subjective rather than objective evidence

  D) confuses the coincidence of two events with a causal relation between the two

  E) depends upon the ambiguous use of a key term

Starting Point Fallacy

This fallacy is closely related to false dilemma. Sometimes, an argument will compare two things in their present state and draw a conclusion about how a course of events has affected them, without considering what differences might have existed between the two things before the course of events began. Committing a **starting point** fallacy is basing a conclusion about two entities upon information gathered at the end of a process, without considering the differences between those entities that existed before the process.

Sample LSAT questions that reflect this fallacy include those in which the conclusion of the argument is properly drawn.

> **Example**: "In a recent study of one hundred overweight individuals, fifty individuals were given only a special diet and fifty individuals were given both a special diet and a rigorous exercise regimen. At the end of the study, all of the individuals had lost weight, with no noticeable difference in weight loss between the two groups. Therefore, a

rigorous exercise regimen has little or no effect on weight loss when combined with the special diet used in the study." The problem with this argument is that we have no information about the differences between those in the first group and those in the second group before the study began. It is possible that the individuals who were diagnosed as needing an exercise regimen were placed in the group that received it, while the others were not. Do not assume that the two groups of individuals started at the same point unless the argument says so.

★ **LSAT EXAM QUESTION**

3.1.12.

Photovoltaic power plants produce electricity from sunlight. As a result of astonishing recent technological advances, the cost of producing electric power at photovoltaic power plants, allowing for both construction and operating costs, is one-tenth of what it was twenty years ago, whereas the corresponding cost for traditional plants, which burn fossil fuels, has increased. Thus, photovoltaic power plants offer a less expensive approach to meeting demand for electricity than do traditional power plants.

(Note that unlike most of the other questions in this chapter, this question asks you to add a sufficient assumption to justify the conclusion.)

16. The conclusion of the argument is properly drawn if which one of the following is assumed?

A) The cost of producing electric power at traditional plants has increased over the past twenty years.

B) Twenty years ago, traditional power plants were producing ten times more electric power than were photovoltaic plants.

C) None of the recent technological advances in producing electric power at photovoltaic plants can be applied to producing power at traditional plants.

D) Twenty years ago, the cost of producing electric power at photovoltaic plants was less than ten times the cost of producing power at traditional plants.

E) The cost of producing electric power at photovoltaic plants is expected to decrease further, while the cost of producing power at traditional plants is not expected to decrease.

Fallacies of Ambiguity

Fallacies of ambiguity all involve wordplay. That is, they involve words that can have multiple meanings, either independently or depending upon the words they are paired with. As you work through LSAT problems (especially Logical Reasoning), beware of ambiguous wording. Your ability to answer the questions correctly will often depend on your awareness of these potential ambiguities.

The following are fallacies of ambiguity:

- equivocation: using a word twice in two different ways
- composition: arguing that a characteristic of the parts is also a characteristic of the whole
- division: arguing that a characteristic of the whole is also a characteristic of the parts

In addition to these specific fallacies of ambiguity, consider the following real-world examples of general ambiguity:

> A sign downtown reads, "CAUTION Slow Resident Parking."

This should be read as "Caution! Slow! Resident parking," but can be erroneously read as "Caution! Slow resident parking."

> A teacher recently posted this Facebook status: "Sign of the times: I'm trying to persuade one of my students not to drop out of school through text messaging."

This is ambiguous because "through text messaging" could modify either the verb *persuade* or the verb phrase *drop out*. That is, the sentence could be read as:

> "I'm trying, through text messaging, to persuade my student not to drop out."
>
> *OR*
>
> "My student is thinking about dropping out of school through text messaging, and I'm trying to persuade him not to."

Context is key to understand meaning.

Equivocation

Whenever a word is used multiple times, there is a chance that it will be used with more than one meaning. The fallacy of **equivocation** occurs when the meaning of a key term illicitly shifts within an argument.

Sample LSAT answer choices that reflect this fallacy include:

- It uses a certain word or term equivocally.
- The argument relies on two different uses of a certain word or term.
- It does not distinguish between two or more senses/meanings of a word or term.

> **Example**: "The media has an obligation to report on whatever is in the public interest. The public interest is clearly focused on the identity of the whistleblower. Therefore, the media has an obligation to report on the identity of the whistleblower." The problem here is that the phrase *public interest* is used twice: first to mean "the public good" and then to mean "what the public wants to hear." This is equivocation.

★ **LSAT EXAM QUESTION**

16.2.15.

The only plants in the garden were tulips, but they were tall tulips. So, the only plants in the garden were tall plants.

(Note that this question asks you to find an answer that has an argument committing the same fallacy as the argument in the preceding passage.)

17. Which one of the following exhibits faulty reasoning most similar to the faulty reasoning in the preceding argument?

    A) The only dogs in the show were poodles, and they were all black poodles. Therefore, all the dogs in the show were black.

    B) All the buildings on the block were tall. The only buildings on the block were office buildings and residential towers. Therefore, all the office buildings on the block were tall buildings.

    C) All the primates in the zoo were gorillas. The only gorillas in the zoo were small gorillas. Therefore, the only primates in the zoo were small primates.

    D) The only fruit in the kitchen was pears, but the pears were not ripe. Thus, none of the fruit in the kitchen was ripe.

    E) All the grand pianos here are large. All the grand pianos here are heavy. Therefore, everything large is heavy.

Composition

The truth of the parts does not necessarily hold true of the whole. Will lightweight parts make a lightweight machine? Do short sentences make short paragraphs? Will exciting chapters make an exciting story? The fallacy of **composition** is arguing that a characteristic of the parts is also a characteristic of the whole.

Sample LSAT answer choices that reflect this fallacy include:
- It makes the unwarranted assumption that what is true of each member of a group, taken separately, is also true of the group as a whole.
- It assumes that because something is true of each of the parts of a whole, it is true of the whole itself.
- It takes for granted that a whole story will have a given characteristic if each of its parts has that characteristic.

> **Example:** "Every member of this band is a superb musician. Therefore, this must be a superb band." This argument is flawed because what is true of the parts (the members being superb) is not necessarily true of the whole (the band). Do not confuse this with a hasty generalization, which would base a conclusion about all band members on a premise about one or a few band members. Composition conclusions, however, are not about the band members but about the actual band as a whole.

★ **LSAT EXAM QUESTION**

6.1.14.

Joshua Smith's new novel was criticized by the book editor for the *Daily Standard* as implausible. That criticism, like so many other criticisms from the same source

---

in the past, is completely unwarranted. As anyone who has actually read the novel would agree, each one of the incidents in which Smith's hero gets involved could very well have happened to someone or another.

18. Which one of the following is the most serious error of reasoning in the argument?

A) It relies on the assumption that a criticism can legitimately be dismissed as unwarranted if it is offered by someone who had previously displayed questionable judgment.

B) It ignores the fact that people can agree about something even though what they agree about is not the case.

C) It calls into question the intellectual integrity of the critic in order to avoid having to address the grounds on which the criticism is based.

D) It takes for granted that a whole story will have a given characteristic if each of its parts has that characteristic.

E) It attempts to justify its conclusion by citing reasons that most people would find plausible only if they were already convinced that the conclusion was true.

Division

Just because something is true of the whole does not mean it will hold true of the parts. Does a heavy machine have to be built from heavy parts? Does a slow fleet of ships have to comprise slow ships? The fallacy of **division** argues that a characteristic of the whole is also a characteristic of the parts.

Sample LSAT answer choices that reflect this fallacy include:

- It assumes what is true of a group as a whole is necessarily true of each member of that group.

- It assumes that what is true of a group of people taken collectively is also true of any individual within that group.

> **Example:** "The student body at this law school takes courses in over twenty disciplines. Margaret is a student at this law school. Therefore, Margaret takes courses in over twenty disciplines." Margaret is a part of the student body, but it is a fallacy to conclude that she individually takes courses in over twenty disciplines, an attribute of the whole group as a collective.

★ LSAT EXAM QUESTION

14.2.14.

The commissioner has announced that Judge Khalid, who was on the seven-member panel appointed to resolve the Amlee labor dispute, will have sole responsibility for resolving the Simdon labor dispute. Since in its decision the Amlee panel showed itself both reasonable and fair, the two sides in the Simdon dispute are undoubtedly justified in the confidence they have expressed in the reasonableness and fairness of the arbitrator assigned to their case.

(Note that this question asks you to find an answer that has an argument committing the same fallacy as the argument in the preceding passage.)

19. Which one of the following contains flawed reasoning most parallel to that contained in the passage?

A) Representing the school board, Marcia Barthes presented to the school's principal a list of recently elected school board members. Since only an elected member of the school board can act as its representative, Ms. Barthes's name undoubtedly appears on that list.

B) Alan Caldalf, who likes being around young children, has decided to become a pediatrician. Since the one characteristic common to all good pediatricians is that they like young children, Mr. Caldalf will undoubtedly be a very good pediatrician.

C) Jorge Diaz is a teacher at a music school nationally known for the excellence of its conducting faculty. Since Mr. Diaz has recently been commended for the excellence of his teaching, he is undoubtedly a member of the school's conducting faculty.

D) Ula Borg, who has sold real estate for Arcande Realty for many years, undoubtedly sold fewer houses last year than she had the year before since the number of houses sold last year by Arcande Realty is far lower than the number sold the previous year.

E) The members of the local historical society unanimously support designating the First National Bank building a historical landmark. Since Evelyn George is a member of that society, she undoubtedly favors according landmark status to the city hall as well.

Fallacies of Formal Logic (Deductive Reasoning)

All these fallacies occur on the LSAT, mostly in Logical Reasoning, though mistaken negation and mistaken reversal may occur in Analytical Reasoning (Logic Games):

The following are fallacies of formal logic (deductive reasoning):

- mistaken reversal: acting as though a condition necessary for an event is sufficient for that event
  - o   If A is true then B is true. B is true.
  - o   Therefore, A is true.

- mistaken negation: acting as though the absence of a sufficient condition for an event precludes that event
  - o   If A is true then B is true. A is false.
  - o   Therefore, B is false.

- either-or fallacy
  - o   Either A is true or B is true. A is true.
  - o   Therefore, B is false.

- undistributed middle
  - o   Some A is B and some A is C. Therefore, some B is C.
      OR

o   All B is A, and some C is A. Therefore, some B is C.

- contradiction
  o   A is true, but A is false.

Mistaken Reversal

"If...then" statements are conditions, not equalities. "If Harry goes to the football game, then it is sunny out" should be drawn as "G → S." Here, the letter *G* stands for "game" in "Harry goes to the game." The letter *S* stands for "sunny" in "it is sunny out." Read this as "If game, then sunny."

Just because it is sunny out, however, does not mean that Harry goes to the football game. That would be "S → G" ("if sunny, then game"). Confusing "G → S" with "S → G" is a **mistaken reversal**.

Sample LSAT answer choices that reflect this fallacy include those that mistake something that is necessary to bring about a situation for something that in itself is enough to bring about that situation.

Example:

If there is an intruder, then the dog barks.   I → B

The dog is barking.   B

Therefore, there must be an intruder.   ∴ I

This argument, like all fallacies, is not valid. It is incorrect to conclude that there must be an intruder based on the two premises given. The dog might be barking for other reasons. This argument is flawed because it mistakes a necessary condition for a sufficient condition. When there is an intruder, it is a necessary condition that the dog is barking. That is, there cannot be an intruder when the dog is not barking. However, the mere fact that the dog is barking is not sufficient to prove that there is an intruder. This argument is flawed because it treats the fact that the dog barking as *necessary* for there to be an intruder *as though it were sufficient to prove* that there is an intruder.

The LSAT will use this "necessary and sufficient" terminology, so be sure this information is clear. You could describe the flaw in the preceding argument in one of two ways:

1. The author mistakes a condition that is necessary for an event with a condition that would be sufficient for that event.

2. The author fails to consider that the dog might bark even when there is no intruder.

Here, Sentence 1 is written in general "logic" terms, while Sentence 2 is written in specific "factual" terms. Look for both general and fact-heavy answer choices.

3.2.7.

To become an expert on a musical instrument, a person must practice. If people practice a musical instrument for three hours each day, they will eventually become experts on that instrument. Therefore, if a person is an expert on a musical instrument, that person must have practiced for at least three hours each day.

20. Which one of the following most accurately describes a flaw in the preceding reasoning?

A) The conclusion fails to take into account that people who practice for three hours every day might not yet have reached a degree of proficiency that everyone would consider expert.

B) The conclusion fails to take into account that practicing for less than three hours each day may be enough for some people to become experts.

C) The conclusion fails to take into account that if a person has not practiced for at least three hours a day, the person has not become an expert.

D) The conclusion fails to take into account that three consecutive hours of daily practice is not recommended by all music teachers.

E) The conclusion fails to take into account that few people have the spare time necessary to devote three hours daily to practice.

Mistaken Negation

As stated earlier, "if...then" statements are conditions, not equalities. "If Harry goes to the football game, then it is sunny out": draw "G → S" (again, read this as "if game, then sunny"). Just because Harry does not go to the football game, however, does not mean that it is not sunny. That would be "~G → ~S" ("if no game, then not sunny"), which is a different statement.

Confusing "G → S" with "~G → ~S" is a **mistaken negation**. Logically, this fallacy is wrong for the same reason as a mistaken reversal: even if it is sunny out, Harry might decide not to go to the game for some other reason. The premise says that Harry's presence at the game guarantees that it is sunny; it does not say that Harry's absence from the game guarantees that it is not sunny.

Sample LSAT answer choices that reflect this fallacy include:

- It assumes without warrant that just because satisfying a given condition is enough to ensure an announcement's importance, satisfying that condition is necessary for its importance.

- The argument fails to establish that a condition under which a phenomenon is said to occur is the only condition under which that phenomenon occurs.

> **Example:**
>
> If there is an intruder, then the dog barks.   I → B
>
> There is no intruder.   ~I
>
> Therefore, the dog is not barking.   ∴ ~B

4.1.8.

Political theorist: The chief foundations of all governments are the legal system and the police force; since there cannot be a good legal system where the police are not well paid, it follows that where the police are well paid, there will be a good legal system.

21. The reasoning in the argument is not sound because it fails to establish that

    A) many governments with bad legal systems have poorly paid police forces.

    B) bad governments with good legal systems must have poorly paid police forces.

    C) a well-paid police force cannot be effective without a good legal system.

    D) a well-paid police force is sufficient to guarantee a good legal system.

    E) some bad governments have good legal systems.

More on Mistaken Reversal and Mistaken Negation

The next few pages explore mistaken reversal and mistaken negation in greater detail. Students frequently struggle with these concepts because colloquial English uses words like *if* and *only if*, so do not feel bad if these fallacies are not intuitive at first.

The two statements—"The dog barks if there is an intruder" and "The dog barks only if there is an intruder"—are **opposite statements**. They have different meanings and are not the same sentence worded in two different ways. However, these sentences are not contradictory. Either of them, or both, may be true in a given situation.

The first statement, "The dog barks if there is an intruder," could also be worded as "If there is an intruder, then the dog barks." In rewording this statement, we are moving the "if" clause from the end of the sentence to the beginning of the sentence. What this means is that the presence of an intruder is sufficient to ensure that the dog will bark. In this situation, an intruder guarantees that the dog will bark. If the dog is not barking, there must not be any intruder. Now let's consider the other statement.

The second statement, "The dog barks only if there is an intruder," means that it is necessary for there to be an intruder in order for the dog to bark. Thus, it is equivalent to "If the dog barks, then there is an intruder." In this case, the dog barking is sufficient to ensure that there is an intruder. In this situation, the presence of an intruder is necessary and must be true in the event that the dog is barking. Therefore, if there is no intruder, then the dog cannot be barking. This has a different meaning than the first sentence.

Neither of the two statements is necessarily true or false, and neither one is necessarily valid or invalid. They are just statements, not arguments. The first statement could be true; it might be the case that your neighbor's dog barks every time there is an intruder, so "If there is an intruder, then the dog barks." This situation does not exclude the possibility that "If the kids are playing, then the dog barks," or "If the dog wants to go out, then the dog barks." If you wanted to convey the idea that the dog will bark every time there is an intruder, you would want to say, "The dog barks if there is an intruder," or one of its equivalents.

The second statement also could be true; it might be the case that your other neighbor's dog has been trained to bark only if there is an intruder. In that case, "If the dog barks, there must be an intruder." This can also be stated, "The dog cannot bark unless there is an intruder." We're not saying that this statement is true about all dogs, but if you do say that this statement is true, then logically you must also agree that its equivalents are all true. Keep in mind that this statement does not ensure that the dog will bark every time there is an intruder. For all we know, the dog never barks, and that would be fully compatible with the statement "The dog barks only if there is an intruder." All this statement is saying is that if the dog is barking, then there must be an intruder. It is impossible, in this situation, for the dog to bark simply because the kids are playing, or because it wants to go out. At a minimum, there would also have to be an intruder for the dog to be barking. If you wanted to convey this set of ideas, then you would want to say, "The dog barks only if there is an intruder," or one of its equivalents.

In Table 2.2, all the statements on the left have the same meaning as each other. All the statements on the right have the same meaning as each other. However, none of the statements on the left share a meaning with the statements on the right.

Very often, people treat sentences like Statement 1 as though they are identical to Statement 2. This usually takes the place of a mistaken reversal or mistaken negation argument. Let's start by looking at Statement 1 and writing out the various valid arguments that you could make from it, and then by writing out the various invalid arguments that people might attempt to make from it. Review formal logic for a refresher on valid and invalid argument patterns of conditional reasoning.

TABLE 2.2. Mistaken Reversal and Mistaken Negation

STATEMENT 1 (All of these statements are equivalent to "The dog barks if there is an intruder.")	STATEMENT 2 (All of these statements are equivalent to "The dog barks only if there is an intruder.")
If there is an intruder, then the dog barks.	If the dog barks, then there is an intruder.
If the dog is not barking, then there is no intruder.	If there is no intruder, then the dog is not barking.
Only if the dog is barking is there an intruder.	Only if there is an intruder does the dog bark.
There cannot be an intruder unless the dog barks.	The dog cannot bark unless there is an intruder.
The dog must be barking or else there would not be an intruder.	There must be an intruder or else the dog would not be barking.

STATEMENT 1 (All of these statements are equivalent to "The dog barks if there is an intruder.")	STATEMENT 2 (All of these statements are equivalent to "The dog barks only if there is an intruder.")
Either the dog is barking or there is no intruder.	Either there is an intruder, or the dog is not barking.
The dog barks if there is an intruder.	There is an intruder if the dog barks.
There is an intruder only if the dog barks.	The dog barks only if there is an intruder.
The presence of an intruder is sufficient to assert that the dog barks.	The dog's barking is sufficient to assert that there is an intruder.
The dog must bark in order for there to be an intruder.	There must be an intruder in order for the dog to bark.
The presence of an intruder ensures that the dog barks.	The dog's barking ensures that there is an intruder.
The presence of an intruder requires that the dog barks.	The dog's barking requires that there is an intruder.

Remember: In any LSAT argument, the premises are never in dispute. Accept them as factually correct. Your goal is simply to analyze whether the conclusion follows logically, based upon the premises. Keep that in mind as we analyze the following arguments.

STATEMENT 1

Remember, we can rearrange the sentence by moving the "If there is an intruder" clause to the beginning of the sentence, without changing the meaning of the sentence.

The dog barks *if* there is an intruder.

If there is an intruder, the dog barks. (I → D)

> **Valid Argument 1, Positive Argument**:
>
> *Premise*: If there is an intruder, then the dog barks. (I → D)
>
> *Premise*: There is an intruder. (I)
>
> *Conclusion*: Therefore, the dog is barking. (∴ D)

This is a valid argument, because the truth of the sufficient condition (an intruder) ensures the truth of the necessary condition (the barking dog).

> **Valid Argument 2, Contrapositive Argument**:
>
> *Premise*: If there is an intruder, then the dog barks. (I → D)
>
> *Premise*: The dog is not barking. (~D [this means "not D"])
>
> *Conclusion*: Therefore, there is no intruder. (∴ ~I)

This is a valid argument because the absence of the necessary condition—the barking dog—ensures that the sufficient condition (the intruder) cannot occur. There is no way that there can be an intruder if the dog is not barking because we have made the absolute statement that if there is an intruder, the dog barks.

> **Invalid Argument 1, Mistaken Reversal:**
>
> *Premise*: If there is an intruder, then the dog barks. (I → D)
>
> *Premise*: The dog is barking. (D)
>
> *Conclusion*: Therefore, there is an intruder. (∴ I)

This is an invalid argument because there may be many other reasons why the dog is barking. Barking is necessary when there is an intruder, but barking is not sufficient to ensure that there is an intruder.

> **Invalid Argument 2, Mistaken Negation:**
>
> *Premise*: If there is an intruder, then the dog barks. (I → D)
>
> *Premise*: There is no intruder. (~I)
>
> *Conclusion*: Therefore, the dog is not barking. (∴ ~D)

This is an invalid argument, because, as earlier, even though there is no intruder there might be other reasons for the dog to bark.

From the same conditional statement, these are two common valid argument patterns (positive and contrapositive) and two common flaws (mistaken reversal and mistaken negation). You will see these patterns on the LSAT. This concept is extremely important because many people do not recognize the error in a mistaken reversal or mistaken negation at first glance. If this concept is intuitive to you, then do not overthink it. Move on to the concepts that are more difficult for you. If this concept is *not* intuitive to you, then you should spend as much time as necessary changing the way that you use conditional reasoning. You want to be able to distinguish a flawed argument from a valid argument.

In the next set of examples, we will look at the valid and invalid arguments that can be made from the alternative statement: "The dog barks only if there is an intruder."

STATEMENT 2

In this scenario, the dog barking *ensures* that there is an intruder. Unlike the earlier situation, which allows other things to be sufficient for the dog to bark, this scenario requires that the dog can only bark if there is an intruder. Therefore, if the dog is barking, there *must* be an intruder. We can also rearrange the original statement:

The dog barks *only if* there is an intruder.

If the dog barks, then there is an intruder. (D → I)

> **Valid Argument 1:**
>
> *Premise*: If the dog barks, then there is an intruder. (D → I)

> *Premise*: The dog is barking. (D)
>
> *Conclusion*: Therefore, there is an intruder. (∴ I)

This is a valid argument because the truth of the sufficient condition (the dog barking) ensures the truth of the necessary condition (the intruder).

> **Valid Argument 2:**
>
> *Premise*: If the dog barks, then there is an intruder. (D → I)
>
> *Premise*: There is no intruder. (~I)
>
> *Conclusion*: Therefore, the dog is not barking. (∴ ~D)

This is a valid argument because the absence of the necessary condition (the intruder) ensures that the sufficient condition (the dog barking) cannot occur.

> **Invalid Argument 1, Mistaken Reversal:**
>
> *Premise*: If the dog barks, then there is an intruder. (D → I)
>
> *Premise*: There is an intruder. (I)
>
> *Conclusion*: Therefore, the dog is barking. (∴ D)

This is invalid because, in this case, the dog *does not have to bark* just because there is an intruder. If the dog is barking, then there must be an intruder, but just because there is an intruder does not mean that the dog will bark. Again, the presence of an intruder is *not sufficient* to ensure that the dog will bark, so even though the dog *may* bark when there is an intruder, one cannot logically conclude that the dog is barking just because there is an intruder.

> **Invalid Argument 2, Mistaken Negation:**
>
> *Premise*: If the dog barks, then there is an intruder. (D → I)
>
> *Premise*: The dog is not barking. (~D)
>
> *Conclusion*: Therefore, there is no intruder. (∴ ~I)

This is invalid for the same reason stated earlier: just because the dog is not barking does not mean that there is no intruder. This is as invalid as saying, "If I have a cold, then I sneeze. I don't have a cold right now. Therefore, I can't sneeze."

So why can't we say that when there is an intruder, the dog barks, and when the dog barks, there is an intruder? Why can't it go both ways?

Well, we can. Often, that is precisely what we want to communicate in day-to-day English, although logically we would need to say something like "The dog barks *if, and only if,* there is an intruder."

This is a combination: "The dog barks if there is an intruder" (meaning "If there is an intruder, then the dog barks") and "The dog barks only if there is an intruder" (meaning "If the dog is barking, then there is an intruder").

If and only if occasionally comes up in Logical Reasoning and Analytical Reasoning (Logic Games). When either of the two conditions is true, then the other must be true. If either condition is false, the other must be false.

When a father tells his son, "You can have your allowance if you take out the trash," odds are he really means "if, and only if." When the son takes out the trash, he is sure to get his allowance, but if the son *does not* take out the trash, he is sure *not* to get his allowance. Only by saying "if and only if" would the father actually be able to convey this message. If the father just says, "You can have your allowance if you take out the trash," then the son might still want to claim his allowance even if he does not take out the trash.

As you hear people use "if" and "only if" in their arguments, pay careful attention to whether they are saying what they mean, and watch out for mistaken reversals and mistaken negations. They are everywhere on the LSAT, in both simple and complex passages, and if you use a mistaken reversal or mistaken negation in your own reasoning, it will likely lead you astray on both the Logical Reasoning and the Logic Games.

Either-or Fallacy

In English, there are two meanings to the word *or*: a strong meaning and a weak meaning. In a sentence like "You can go either to Paris or to London," there is a strong *or*, because the choice between Paris and London is exclusive (by choosing Paris, you choose "not London," and vice versa). Thus, the statement "either A or B is true" is strong; *or* would prevent you from choosing both A and B.

Most of the time, however, English uses a weak *or*, which does allow both A and B to be true. Consider the sentence "You must take either French or Spanish in order to graduate." It is certain that you will choose either French or Spanish. But it is certainly possible that you may take both.

On the LSAT, you should assume that all instances of the word *or* are this weak *or*. Given the statement, "Either A is true or B is true," it is a fallacy to argue, "A is true, so B is false." The only valid arguments you could make are "A is false, so B is true," or "B is false, so A is true."

Note that this fallacy is different from false dilemma. A false dilemma may artificially *create* an either-or statement. The **either-or** fallacy occurs in an argument that takes an either-or statement as its premise.

Definition: Wrongly concluding that two alternatives are mutually exclusive merely because one of the two alternatives must be true.

> **Example**: "Burger Palace franchises are required to serve either Coke or Pepsi. The franchise in Miami is serving Coke. So, they must not be serving Pepsi." This is fallacious because the store might be serving both Coke and Pepsi.

This fallacy tends to occur within passages that do not accompany "argument flaw" Logical Reasoning questions. Understanding this fallacy is crucial to understanding the use of the word *or* on both Logical Reasoning and Logic Games, but this is perhaps the least common of the fallacies in this chapter.

The Undistributed Middle

When two groups share a characteristic, it is a fallacy to assume that the two groups must therefore have common members. Humans have ears and elephants have ears, but no human is an elephant.

In other words, when one group has members in common with each of two other groups, those two groups do not necessarily have members in common with each other. Things with ears include both humans and elephants, but no human is an elephant. These are two ways of thinking about this fallacy.

Sample LSAT answer choices that reflect this fallacy include those that fail to recognize that one set might have some members in common with each of two others even though those two other sets have no members in common with each other.

> **Example**: "All roses are plants. Some plants are poisonous. Thus, some roses are poisonous." This example takes the form "All A is B, some B is C; therefore, some A is C." This form is always flawed.

★ LSAT EXAM QUESTION

2.1.20.

All savings accounts are interest-bearing accounts. The interest from some interest-bearing accounts is tax free, so there must be some savings accounts that have tax-free interest.

(Note that this question asks you to find an answer with an argument committing the same fallacy as the argument in the preceding passage.)

22. Which one of the following arguments is flawed in a way most similar to the way in which the passage is flawed?

   A) All artists are intellectuals. Some great photographers are artists. Therefore, some great photographers must be intellectuals.

   B) All great photographers are artists. All artists are intellectuals. Therefore, some great photographers must be intellectuals.

   C) All great photographers are artists. Some artists are intellectuals. Therefore, some great photographers are intellectuals.

   D) All great photographers are artists. Some great photographers are intellectuals. Therefore, some artists must be intellectuals.

   E) All great photographers are artists. No artists are intellectuals. Therefore, some great photographers must not be intellectuals.

Contradiction

Last of all is the most straightforward of the fallacies, **contradiction**: the assertion of two statements that cannot both be true at the same time. When you see the word *incompatible*, meaning that certain propositions cannot be simultaneously true, think "contradictory."

Sample LSAT answer choices that reflect this fallacy include:

- Information was introduced that actually contradicts the conclusion.

- The conclusion contradicts the claim of the speakers.
- The results of an analysis are interpreted as indicating that the use of the substance both was, and was not, extremely restricted.

> **Example:** "The evidence that we caused a greater net increase in jobs than the previous administration is clear: we reduced the rate of unemployment growth per year from 10 percent to only 3 percent." This is contradictory, because the premise indicates that unemployment is still increasing, while the conclusion claims a net increase in jobs (that is, a decrease in employment).

★ **LSAT EXAM QUESTION**

2.1.5.

A gas tax of one cent per gallon would raise one billion dollars per year at current consumption rates. Since a tax of fifty cents per gallon would therefore raise fifty billion dollars per year, it seems a perfect way to deal with the federal budget deficit. This tax would have the additional advantage that the resulting drop in the demand for gasoline would be ecologically sound and would keep our country from being too dependent on foreign oil producers.

23. Which one of the following most clearly identifies an error in the author's reasoning?

    A) The author cites irrelevant data.

    B) The author relies on incorrect current consumption figures.

    C) The author makes incompatible assumptions.

    D) The author mistakes an effect for a cause.

    E) The author appeals to conscience rather than reason.

Answer Key

Questions marked with a star are official LSAT questions provided by the LSAC.

★ **1.** **B) is correct.** This is the definition of appeal to emotion. This is the right answer. A) is the definition of circular reasoning, which is incorrect. C) is an example of a red herring; it does not occur in this argument. D) is the definition of an ad hominem attack/argument against the person, which is not the fallacy here. E) is the definition of false cause, which does not apply here either.

Instead of making a rational argument as to why she should collect her son's insurance policy, the mother says she is ill and has no other support, making an emotional appeal. These arguments are intended to tug on the heartstrings of their recipients, but they do not appeal to reason.

Be sure to separate logic and emotion. It is not necessarily illogical to take an action based on an emotional response. In some situations, people make a logical choice to act based on an emotional stimulus. The key is having the right premise to justify a conclusion drawn on the basis of an emotional appeal.

For example, add this premise to the preceding LSAT argument: "When someone is ill and has no other support, companies should deviate from the rules and render a decision that favors that individual."

Now, is it likely that the insurance company would adopt this premise? No, of course not. But if it did, then you could read the remaining premises in the argument and logically arrive at the conclusion that the mother should receive her insurance benefits.

As you will see, most fallacies of inductive reasoning can be cured by adding the proper premise to justify the conclusion. The arguments in the passages are flawed, but they are not *fatally* flawed.

★ **2.** **A) is correct.** This is the definition of an ad hominem attack—an argument against the person. B) is the definition of circular reasoning and is incorrect. C) is an example of ambiguity and does not actually occur in this argument. D) is the definition of straw man and is incorrect. E) is the definition of equivocation and is incorrect.

Here, the conclusion of the argument was the first sentence: "The proposal to give students greater choice should be abandoned." But what were the premises? The premises only offered evidence about the characteristics of the students behind the proposal. No premise addressed the conclusion. This is a classic attack on the person.

★ **3.** **E) is correct.** This is an example of false analogy. Maxwell, Newton, and Einstein received funding and produced beneficial research for the world, but that does not necessarily justify funding for the observatory director. An analogy is only strong if there are premises supporting the comparison. A) is an example of an inappropriate appeal to authority, which is not the fallacy here. B) is incorrect. There is no need to know who opposes the development of the mega-telescope; the issue is why the observatory director should receive funding. Rather than analyzing whether the premises given lead to the conclusion given, readers start thinking about what they would want to know in real life about a request to fund this sort of proposal. Avoid the impulse to bring in such outside considerations. C) is an example of an ad hominem attack, which does not apply here. D) is an example of equivocation, which is incorrect.

★ 4. **B) is correct.** This choice explains a red herring, which is the fallacy here. A) is not a fallacy. C) is an unjustified assumption, but it is not correct. The supplier does not assume that the office manager cares about the environment; instead, the supplier gives a response that addresses the historical reputation of recycled paper. D) is also an unjustified assumption and is incorrect. Nowhere does the supplier make an argument that assumes the office manager understands paper manufacturing technology. E) is an example of missing the point, which is not the fallacy here.

Answer Choices That Are Always Wrong: What would make answer choice E) a fallacy of missing the point? If it said, "It ignores the office manager's concern about quality," that would describe a mistaken conclusion. However, adding the word *legitimate* in this answer choice places it in the category of answer choices that are always wrong. This answer and answers like it are always wrong because they go beyond merely describing a logical shortcoming; they introduce a factual challenge. Who determines whether a concern about paper quality is "legitimate"? This answer choice imposes a subjective value judgment on the situation, and a correct answer will not do that. Instead, it will limit itself to the logical gap in the argument's reasoning.

Red Herring Versus Missing the Point: Note that the supplier is not missing the point in the preceding question. His argument intends to disprove the office manager's argument, so it is not the supplier's conclusion that is irrelevant. Instead, it is the supplier's facts about the historical origins of paper that are irrelevant as support for the conclusion given. The fact that recycled paper has been valued historically does not prove that recycled paper is not inferior to the other types of paper currently available.

★ 5. **C) is correct.** This choice is an example of straw man, which is the fallacy here. A) is not a fallacy; it is a challenge to the student's premise. B) sounds like an unjustified assumption. This fallacy does not occur here, but the answer choice would be describing a situation where the dean wrongly assumes that speech is different from other behavior in certain respects. D) is an ad hominem attack/argument against the person, which is not the fallacy here. E) is the definition of an appeal to force, which is a subset of appeal to emotion.

The student representative was arguing that the university was wrong to expel a student for verbal harassment. But the dean distorts this argument from "you should not have penalized him for verbal harassment" to "you should endorse verbal harassment." It is much easier to defeat the argument "you should endorse verbal harassment" than it is to defeat what the representative said.

DID YOU KNOW?

A red herring contains an irrelevant or mistaken premise. Missing the point contains an irrelevant or mistaken conclusion.

HELPFUL HINT

The odds are that you know people who make straw man arguments on a regular basis. Over the next week, every time you hear two people engaging in conversation or debate, listen for a straw man.

★ 6. **D) is correct.** The argument fails to rule out the possibility that the school hires a greater number of part-time teachers. If the argument had ruled out that possibility (presumably by telling us that the school hires at least as many full-time teachers as part-time teachers), then it would have avoided the fallacy.

This set of answers differs from those we have seen so far because the answers are not generic logical terms. Rather, these answers are stated in terms of the argument's facts. The correct answer identifies the leap that the argument is taking from its premises to its conclusion.

What are our premises?

One-quarter of part-time teachers now quit.

One-third of full-time teachers now quit.

So, as a percentage within each group, we know that relatively more full-time teachers quit than part-time teachers.

But what is the argument's conclusion? That more full-time teachers quit than part-time teachers. This conclusion is in absolute terms, and that is a problem.

If we knew that there were an equal number of part-time and full-time teachers, then certainly the conclusion would follow, but that information has not been given to us. What if there were one thousand part-time teachers and one hundred full-time teachers? Then more part-time teachers would have quit than full-time teachers.

The premises and the conclusion are disconnected in these arguments. In these examples, the conclusion is in different terms than what the premises will logically support.

★ 7. **D) is correct.** The premise of the argument is that seven out of ten shoppers prefer Northwoods, but we do not know why they prefer it. Nevertheless, the argument's conclusion is that Northwoods is "tops for taste" (tastes the best). This argument jumps from Northwoods being preferred to Northwoods tasting the best, missing the point. A) does not indicate a fallacy. In fact, knowing that a small proportion of shoppers expressed no preference is useful. It indicates that most of the shoppers surveyed did express a preference, validating the survey. B) is irrelevant; the argument does not assume that only Northwoods is made the old-fashioned way. C) is irrelevant because the argument does not assume that the number of shoppers surveyed was larger than a "sizable minority" of the total population. E) is irrelevant because the argument is limited to a discussion of maple syrup. It does not matter whether shoppers buy other kinds of syrup.

★ 8. **E) is correct.** This is the definition of argument from ignorance, and thus is the correct answer. The premise is the absence of evidence that food irradiation is unsafe; the conclusion is that food irradiation is therefore safe. A) is not a fallacy. The scientists' motive is not an issue in this argument. B) is not a fallacy. Having an interest in the conclusion you are proving is not a fatal flaw. C) is not a fallacy. Whether there are other objections to irradiation is irrelevant. D) is not a fallacy. Logic does not require a minimum level of detail in any argument.

★ 9. In this argument, the fallacy was appealing to the authority of the museum's night security guard without justifying why he is authoritative. What if he was asleep or incompetent? "The museum's night security guard maintains" should be a red flag that this is the fallacy. You are looking for an argument that makes a similarly inappropriate appeal to authority.

B) is correct. How do the store's competitors know whether the store made a profit or broke even? This is the same inappropriate appeal to authority. A) is flawed because the winner could have had the highest overall score without having the highest score in either individual category. This is a nuanced example of composition. C) is an example of numbers and proportions. The argument jumps from percentage married to absolute numbers overall. D) is an example of missing the point. The argument jumps from humans and pets to wild animals without providing justification. E) is an example of unjustified assumption. The argument assumes that the late questionnaires will be processed but does not justify such an assumption.

★ 10. **E) is correct.** By presenting an alternate possible cause—overeating—this choice shows that there is more than one way to explain the effect (the illness), and that it was a fallacy for the argument to arbitrarily choose the cause it did (the hot peppers). A) is an example of hasty generalization, which is not the fallacy here. B) does not really describe a false cause argument. Instead, it describes a missing-the-point situation where the author jumps to a conclusion without proving the premises needed to get there. C) is not a fallacy. Whether Monroe desires to continue eating at Tip Top does not help determine the cause of his illness. D) is not a fallacy. This argument does not require proving that everyone who ate the peppers became ill in order to prove that the hot peppers made Monroe ill.

★ 11. **A) is correct.** This is an example of hasty generalization. Just because the professor's students have turned in poor writing this year does not mean college students generally write worse than they used to. B) is nearly a description of an inappropriate appeal to authority, although it is not unreasonable to expect that a professor may judge her own students' writing ability. C) is irrelevant; the professor is not arguing why her students are poor writers. This argument is merely concluding that college students write worse than they used to. D) is a form of missing the point, which is not the fallacy here. E) is an example of equivocation, as might arise when a key term has multiple possible meanings.

★ 12. This argument starts with a generalization: "On average, drivers who use the new system have a better on-time record than drivers who use the old system." Just because Millicent Smith has the best on-time record, however, does not mean she is on the new system. She could be the exception to the rule. We are looking for a similar pattern of argumentation in an answer.

C) is correct. The first clause of the second sentence is the generalization here. (Remember, the order of the propositions in the argument does not matter.) Just because "this tomato" is the largest of the crop does not mean it was grown in the experimental crop. It could be the exception to the rule. A) is a valid argument, not flawed reasoning. "This vehicle" cannot be among the vehicles acquired before 1988, or else the first sentence of the argument would be false. B) is flawed, but it is also backward. If this argument first told us that Henri was the tallest soccer player of either team and then concluded that Henri must therefore belong to the blue team, it would be a match. D) is incorrect: the generalization (the first sentence) is the conclusion of the argument, rather than a premise. E) is an example of confusing absolute and relative terms. We can logically conclude that the lawn mower will probably require more maintenance than most electric mowers, but we cannot conclude that it will require "a lot" of maintenance.

★ 13. **E) is correct.** This identifies the unjustified assumption in this passage and is thus the correct answer. The argument says that achieving the goal requires knowledge of neurons and their functions, knowledge of how neurons interact, and distinguishing the psychological faculties to be explained. However, only the first and third are stated as being possible. The argument assumes without justification that the second is possible as well. A) is an example of contradiction, which is not the fallacy here. B) is not a fallacy. Logic does not require a minimum level of detail in any argument. C) is an example of equivocation, which is not the fallacy here. D) is irrelevant because the issue is whether it will be possible to explain mental functions in neurobiological terms, not whether it would be useful.

★ 14. **C) is correct.** Circular reasoning is the fallacy here. The conclusion states that Cotrell is average at best, but one of the premises is that Cotrell cannot write better than average: a classic example of circular reasoning. A) is an example of missing the point, B) and E) are examples of hasty generalization, and D) is an example of an inappropriate appeal to authority. None of these is the fallacy here.

★ 15. **B) is correct.** This is the definition of false dilemma and is the correct answer. The argument only addresses assignments that are too difficult or unchallenging. These premises are misleading because they do not address assignments that are appropriately challenging. A) is an example of missing the point (*non sequitur*), D) is the definition of false cause, and E) is the definition of equivocation. None of these is the fallacy here. C) is not a fallacy at all.

★ 16. First, let's parse out the propositions in this argument:

Premise: Photovoltaic (PV) electric power costs one-tenth of what it cost twenty years ago.

Premise: Traditional energy has increased in cost.

Conclusion: Therefore, PV electric power is cheaper than traditional energy.

We know that, over the past twenty years, PV electric power has gotten cheaper while traditional energy has gotten more expensive, but we do not know how much either of them cost to begin with. What if PV electric power cost ten dollars twenty years ago, such that today it costs one dollar and traditional energy once cost five cents and now it costs six cents? Without knowing the starting point, it is impossible to draw a comparison between the cost of PV electric power and traditional energy on the basis of the information given.

Now let's figure out how to answer the question. Our job here is to add a sufficient assumption (see the following chart for more information on this question type). A sufficient assumption will, as an additional premise, make our conclusion follow with 100 percent certainty. Remember, the question told us to assume that the answer *is* true. So, with that in mind, we want an answer that will allow us to read the premises and conclusively assert that PV electric power is cheaper than traditional energy. As noted, this will require knowing something about the starting price before the prices changed.

D) is correct. Twenty years ago, PV electric power cost less than ten times what traditional energy cost. If we then read our premises, which say that PV electric power today costs one-tenth of what it cost twenty years ago, and that traditional energy has meanwhile increased in cost, then we know for sure that PV electric power is cheaper today than traditional energy. Let's demonstrate with numbers, assuming that traditional energy cost one dollar twenty years ago:

	Twenty Years Ago	Today
Traditional Energy	$1	More than $1
PV Electric Power	Less than $10	Less than $1

First, we know that twenty years ago, PV electric power would have cost less than ten dollars, since our answer choice is telling us that it cost less than ten times what traditional energy cost. Then, we read our premise that says PV electric power costs one-tenth of what it cost twenty years ago; if it used to cost less than ten dollars, then it now costs less than one dollar.

Finally, we read our premise that says the cost of traditional energy has increased; if it used to cost one dollar, now it costs more than one dollar. This proves that adding answer D) is sufficient to justify our conclusion with 100 percent certainty. Regardless of how much traditional energy cost twenty years ago, the result will be the same: it now costs more than PV electric power.

A) does not allow us to compare the costs of PV electric power with traditional energy. It only tells us that it is more expensive for traditional plants to produce electric power. B) tells us how much power the plants were producing, but nothing about cost. C) discusses technological advances, but again, nothing about cost. E) discusses future predictions, but nothing about present or past cost.

17. ★ **C) is correct.** This is the right answer and is an exact match: *Small* is the ambiguous term here. Small gorillas are not necessarily small primates. A) is a perfectly valid argument, so it is incorrect. There is no ambiguity here because the meaning of *black* does not change depending on the word it modifies. B) is also a valid argument (a valid, positive-mixed hypothetical). If the building is on the block, then it is a tall building. Office buildings and residential towers were on the block. Therefore, the office buildings on the block were tall buildings. D) is a valid deductive argument, too. If fruit is in the kitchen, it must be pears. The pears are not ripe. Therefore, none of the fruit in the kitchen is ripe. E) is an example of the undistributed middle, but it is not the fallacy here.

 **HELPFUL HINT**

Here, the word "tall" is ambiguous because its meaning is relative to the word it modifies; a tall tulip may not necessarily be a tall plant.

18. ★ **D) is correct.** This choice is an example of the fallacy of composition and is the correct answer. Just because the parts of the story (the incidents) are plausible does not make the book itself plausible. A) and C) are examples of an attack on/argument against the person (*ad hominem*). B) is an example of missing the point. (People cannot agree about this course of action because it is not happening.) E) is an example of circular reasoning. This answer choice is describing an argument that attempts to prove its conclusion by citing premises that, in turn, depend upon the truth of the conclusion.

19. ★ **D) is correct.** The argument concludes that Khalid will be a fair arbitrator in the Simdon dispute because he was on the Amlee panel, and the Amlee panel as a whole was reasonable and fair. Here, the whole is the Amlee panel and the part is Khalid. Just because the whole was fair does not mean the part is fair. In D), the whole is Arcande Realty, and the part is Ula Borg. Arcande may have sold fewer houses, but Ula Borg may have sold more houses. A) is an example of unjustified assumption; it assumes that Ms. Barthes was recently elected. B) is a mistaken reversal. Even if someone likes young children, and all good pediatricians like young children, that does not mean that the person will be a good pediatrician. C) is an example of the undistributed middle. Mr. Diaz may have excellent teaching, and the school may have excellent conducting faculty, but there is not necessarily overlap between Mr. Diaz and the conducting faculty. E) is the trap answer: if the historical society unanimously supports something, then all its members must have supported it as well. The other problem with this answer is that it misses the point when it jumps from designating the bank to designating city hall.

20. ★ You may have diagrammed the conditional statements in the argument like this:

If expert, then practice. $E \rightarrow P$

If three hours, then expert. $3 \rightarrow E$

Therefore, if expert, then three hours. $\therefore E \rightarrow 3$

Practicing for three hours, according to the premise, is certainly sufficient to become an expert. The problem is that the conclusion says that practicing for three hours is a necessary condition for becoming an expert. This is a mistaken reversal because it ignores the possibility that there may be other ways to become an expert besides practicing for three hours a day.

B) is correct. Three hours of practice a day is sufficient to become an expert (meaning, three hours of practice guarantees that you will become an expert), but we cannot conclude that it is necessary. For all we know, people can become experts by practicing for ten minutes a day. A) is not a fallacy; the passage says three hours of practice every day ensures that you will become an expert. Whether some people consider this level of expertise inadequate is irrelevant to this argument. C) is not a fallacy. This answer choice is essentially saying that the conclusion has failed to take into account the conclusion. The statement in this answer choice (if a person has not practiced for at least three hours a day, the person has not become an expert) is the contrapositive of the argument's conclusion (if a person is an expert on a musical instrument, that person must have practiced for at least three hours each day). D) is irrelevant because the argument does not depend on the agreed recommendation of "all music teachers." This answer choice attempts to make a factual challenge against the argument. E) is also irrelevant and not a fallacy. Whether people have spare time is not an element of the argument.

★ 21.   **D) is correct.** The premise here is "where the police are not well paid, there cannot be a good legal system," and the conclusion is "where the police are well paid, there will be a good legal system." This is a clear example of a mistaken negation: without well-paid police, the legal system is bad. However, just because there are well-paid police does not necessarily mean the legal system will be good. It might still be bad for some other reason. The answer must show that the argument has failed to establish that a well-paid police force ensures a good legal system. D) asserts that the argument has failed to establish its conclusion. Specifically, the argument has failed to establish the conditional relationship in the conclusion. A) is irrelevant; there is no need to establish the reason behind why "many governments" may have bad legal systems. B) does not make sense in light of the passage. If the government had a good legal system, then it would not have a poorly paid legal force. Also, this argument is talking about bad *governments*, which is not the issue here. C) is talking about effectiveness, and E) is talking about bad governments, not the issue.

★ 22.   This passage is in the form of "All S are I. Some I is T; therefore, some S is T," which is the same as "All A is B, some B is C; therefore, some A is C." This is the classic undistributed middle.

Just because some interest-bearing accounts are tax free does not mean that those are the same accounts as the savings accounts that bear interest. For all we know, every interest-bearing account, *except* interest-bearing savings accounts, is tax free. See the following visual diagram. Savings accounts and tax-free interest do not *necessarily have to* overlap.

A) is incorrect. This is a valid argument, so it cannot be the right answer. This argument is in the form "All A is B, some C is A; therefore, some C is B."

B) is incorrect. This is a valid argument, so it cannot be the right answer. This argument is in the form "All A is B, all B is C; therefore, some A is C." (Note: it would also be valid to conclude that "All great photographers are intellectuals, but it is certainly valid to conclude that some are.")

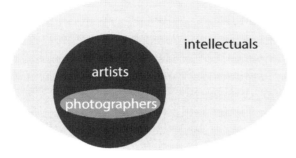

C) is correct. Where A = great photographers, B = artists, and C = intellectuals, the pattern of this argument is "All A is B, some B is C; therefore, some A is C." Notice how in the diagram, great photographers can be artists without overlapping with intellectuals.

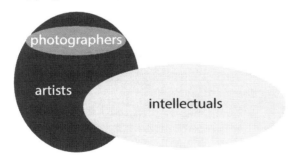

D) is incorrect. This is a valid argument, so it cannot be the right answer. This argument is in the form "All A is B, some A is C; therefore, some B is C." This is identical to answer A), with the exception that the "some" statements are given in reverse. For example, A) says "some C is A," whereas D) says "some A is C"—an irrelevant distinction because the two statements are the same.

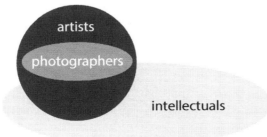

E) is incorrect. This is a valid argument, so it cannot be the right answer. This argument is in the form "All A is B, all B is not C; therefore, some A is not C." This is identical to answer B), with the exception that this answer has "not" statements. (Note: it would also be valid to conclude here that "No great photographers are intellectuals.")

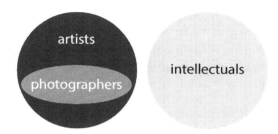

★ 23.   **C) is correct.** This is an example of contradiction. The author assumes that raising the gasoline tax will not affect the demand for gasoline (this is a necessary assumption, because he argues that the taxes collected will rise proportionally to the amount of the tax levied). Then, in the next sentence, the author states that there will be a drop in demand. It is contradictory to assume that demand will both stay the same and decrease at the same time; such statements cannot both be simultaneously true. A) is the definition of red herring, which is not the fallacy here. B) is not a fallacy; it attempts to bring a factual challenge against the accuracy of the consumption figures, but you (the reader) have no basis for determining a consumption figure's accuracy. On "argument flaw" questions, leave your outside premises at home and stick to analyzing the argument's reasoning. D) is the definition of false cause, and E) is the definition of appeal to emotion. Neither is the fallacy here.

3 | Logical Reasoning: Questions

Question Types: An Overview

There are eighteen types of Logical Reasoning questions on the LSAT, organized into four broader thematic families.

The eighteen question types are as follows:

1. Main Conclusion
2. Inference (Must Be True/Must Be False)
3. Inference (Most Strongly Supported)
4. Necessary Assumption
5. Point at Issue
6. Underlying Principle
7. Principle Application
8. Strengthen
9. Weaken
10. Justify (Sufficient Assumption)
11. Resolve
12. Method of Reasoning
13. Role of a Statement
14. Argument Flaw
15. Evaluate the Argument
16. Parallel Reasoning
17. Parallel Flaw
18. Parallel Principle

The four thematic families follow:

1. Passage-Based questions
2. Hypothetical questions
3. Critical Reasoning questions
4. Parallel Reasoning questions

Within each family, the same general strategies apply.

Over the next set of pages, we will examine each of the eighteen Logical Reasoning question types in detail, looking at

- tips for solving the questions.
- how to identify the question type.
- how to read the passage that accompanies the question type.
- how to anticipate the answer.
- common misconceptions.
- an actual LSAT question, with an answer explanation.

As you work through these pages, read the information on each question type and then attempt to solve the question before checking the answer.

Once you have worked through the question types, try your hand at the full-length section of Logical Reasoning questions. You may choose to complete the section timed—in which case you have thirty-five minutes for twenty-six questions—or untimed, although you should not take longer than fifty minutes to an hour under any circumstances. Then review your answers and reread the portions of this book that are relevant to the questions you miss. You want to be able to explain exactly why each wrong answer is wrong, and exactly why each right answer is right, all through natural language.

Strategies for Solving Logical Reasoning Questions

Table 3.1 identifies the components of a Logical Reasoning question.

TABLE 3.1. Components of a Logical Reasoning Question

COMPONENT	EXAMPLE
Source: For official LSAT questions, the PrepTest number from which the question is taken is listed here for your reference.	★ LSAT Exam Question (from PrepTest 12, LR 2)
Passage: Each passage consists of one sentence to one paragraph of text and is followed by one or two questions. In recent tests, each passage generally has its own question. There are twenty-four to twenty-six questions per thirty-five-minute Logical Reasoning section. Most passages are not mere information; instead, they are arguments in which you should identify the conclusion separately from premises and background information. The conclusion may be anywhere in the passage. Some passages (specifically those accompanying Inference or Resolve questions) may contain only a set of facts rather than an argument, but this is not the norm.	10. Household indebtedness, which some theorists regard as causing recession, was high preceding the recent recession, but so was the value of assets owned by households. Admittedly, if most of the assets were owned by quite affluent households, and most of the debt was owned by low-income households, high household debt levels could have been the cause of the recession despite high asset values; low-income households might have been decreased spending in order to pay off debts, while the quite affluent ones might simply have failed to increase spending. But, in fact, quite affluent people must have owed most of the household debt, since money is not lent to those without assets. Therefore, the real cause must lie elsewhere.

COMPONENT	EXAMPLE
Question: Many distinct types of questions are discussed in this chapter. Read the question carefully and answer exactly what is asked. For most students, it is best to know the question before reading the passage so that you know what to look for as you read.	The argument is structured to lead to which one of the following conclusions?
Answers: Each question will have five answer choices. One is correct, while the other four are wrong. On many difficult questions, you may find two answers that seem to be correct. Rather than choosing the answer that "sounds the best," look for why one of the two answers is incorrect and eliminate it.	A) High levels of household debt did not cause the recent recession. B) Low-income households succeeded in paying off their debts despite the recent recession. C) Affluent people probably increased their spending levels during the recent recession. D) High levels of household debt have little impact on the economy. E) When people borrowed money prior to the recent recession, they did not use it to purchase assets.

For each question, the following method is suggested:

1. Read the question (five seconds).

2. Read the passage, paraphrasing to yourself as you read. Identify any conclusions (ten to thirty seconds).

3. Stop and anticipate the answer (ten to twenty seconds).

4. Glance through the answers, looking for one similar to your anticipated answer (ten seconds).

5. Read the most plausible answer(s) more carefully, looking back to the passage, if needed, to confirm that your answer is correct, and all others are wrong (ten to twenty seconds).

These steps are discussed in greater detail on the following pages. Before continuing, you may wish to attempt the sample question in Table 3.1, which will be explained along the way.

Read the Question

Practice reading the question before you read the passage. Some experts recommend reading the passage before the question. Their argument is that if you read the question first, you will end up having to read it again after you read the passage. This is true.

 HELPFUL HINT

The various question types are explained throughout this chapter. As you work through the chapter, develop a firm grasp of what each question is asking so that you can avoid potential traps.

However, if you read the passage first, you will likely find yourself having to read the entire passage *again* after you read the question, which will take even more time. Unless you have an outstanding memory, you will likely have to read something twice; by reading the question before the passage, you will get more out of your initial reading of the passage, and you will minimize the quantity of material that you reread.

Read the Passage

As you read, paraphrase what you are reading, rather than focusing on every word of the passage:

- Pay more attention to the structure of the passage than to the content. Your job is to assess the logical soundness of the passage, *not* the factual soundness. Ignore factual truth.

- Identify the author's conclusion(s). Read the conclusion, and then read the premises. Do the premises support the conclusion? If not, why?

- Notice conditional statements, and diagram them in the margin as you read.

- Watch out for extreme language in conclusions.

- Look for language gaps between the premises and the conclusion. For example, if the premises support a conclusion about monkeys, but the conclusion itself says primates, this may be a weak point that is relevant to answering the question.

Table 3.2 illustrates how you might read the sample passage presented in Table 3.1.

TABLE 3.2. Paraphrasing Passages	
ORIGINAL PASSAGE	**YOUR (SILENT) PARAPHRASE**
10. Household indebtedness, which some theorists regard as causing recession, was high preceding the recent recession, but so was the value of assets owned by households. Admittedly, if most of the assets were owned by quite affluent households, and most of the debt was owned by low-income households, high household debt levels could have been the cause of the recession despite high asset values; low-income households might have been decreased spending in order to pay off debts, while the quite affluent ones might simply have failed to increase spending. But, in fact, quite affluent people must have owed most of the household debt, since money is not lent to those without assets. Therefore, the real cause must lie elsewhere.	• Some think debt caused the recession. Debt was high. • But assets were high too. • (Sounds like the author's conclusion is "Debt didn't cause the recession.") • If the rich owned the assets and the poor owned the debt, then debt might have been the cause. • [details, come back if necessary] • But the poor cannot acquire debt, so the rich must have owned most of the debt. • Therefore, the cause of the recession is something other than debt.

The question asked, "The argument is structured to lead to which one of the following conclusions?" This tells you that your task is to come up with the author's conclusion (review premise/conclusion). As you read the passage, notice the general structure of the passage:

- Some people think that *x* is true.

- But… [details].

- Also, *x* could be true if *y* were true. But *y* isn't true. Therefore, *x* isn't true.

Frequently, Logical Reasoning passages follow the pattern of "Some people think *x*, but…" In almost every circumstance, regardless of what follows in the passage, the author's point in such an argument is simply that *x* is false.

Here, the author tells us that some theorists blame household debt for the recession, but [additional details]. This tells us, before we even get past the first sentence, that the author's point is very likely: "Household debt did not cause the recession." The author confirms this for us in the last sentence of the passage.

As you read, pay more attention to the structure and logical flow of the argument than to the factual details. Nobody is testing you on whether the poor can acquire enough debt to cause a recession. Whether that is true or false in real life is irrelevant to your task. You are to identify the argument's conclusion, so stay focused on the task at hand.

Stop and Anticipate the Answer

This is the most important step. Students who score high on the LSAT are almost always able to stop at the end of a question and express a possible answer in natural, everyday language. You will not necessarily be able to guess the correct answer word for word, but you must allow your brain to consider how the right answer will probably look.

If you skip this step, you risk becoming distracted by the five answer choices, many of which may include enticing language and factual details from the passage. You will see language in the answer choices that you recognize from the passage. An irrelevant answer choice can seem correct, simply because of the way it is worded or because it does include facts from the passage. Take heed: always stop and anticipate the answer.

In the sample question in Table 3.1, you would anticipate "Debt did not cause the recession" as the answer.

Glance Through the Answers

Spend ten seconds or so glancing through the five answer choices. Keep your eyes open for answers that resemble your anticipated answer. Crossing out obviously incorrect answers, while lightly marking those that appear correct, can also be helpful.

Select the Correct Answer

If you have two or three possible answers, do NOT pick an answer for any of the following reasons:

- It is the shortest.

- It is the longest.

- It has the most straightforward wording.

- It has the most complicated wording. (Incidentally, no LSAT answer is incorrect because it seems too easy.)

- It states a phrase, clause, or sentence word for word as it appears in the passage.

- It does not state a phrase, clause, or sentence word for word as it appears in the passage.

- It would give you an even number of C) or D) answers (or some other answer choice letter). Out of twenty-five questions, there will not necessarily be five each of A), B), C), D), and E). In fact, there might be as few as two or as many as ten of a given letter in any given question set. Additionally, you might have up to four in a row of the same letter. Do not base your answer on superstition.

In short, do not pick an answer just because it sounds or looks good. Instead, look for reasons to eliminate answers that are incorrect.

For example, you should eliminate an answer if:

- its language is more extreme than it should be.

- you would have to bring in outside information to justify the answer as correct.

- it discusses a topic that is (even slightly) different from the topic at hand.

No LSAT questions will require you to pick the better of two good answer choices. There will always be four answers that are clearly wrong for an identifiable reason.

It may be extremely difficult to determine why an answer is wrong, so develop your ability to identify the reasons why answer choices are incorrect. If this seems difficult, try taking an LSAT PrepTest or two and simply read through the questions and answers (with the right answers circled). Spend several hours studying each test until you can extract and explain why each right answer is right and why each wrong answer is wrong.

Time Management/Section Practice

You will have thirty-five minutes to answer between twenty-four and twenty-six Logical Reasoning questions. This allows you one minute and twenty seconds to one minute and twenty-seven seconds per question.

Within each section, the easiest questions tend to fall within the first ten questions, and the hardest between questions 12 and 22. Do not mistake this for an easy-to-hard progression. The first question may be very difficult, and a later question may be very straightforward. This pattern has never been officially announced by LSAC, but observers have spotted it on modern LSATs since the early 1990s. Accordingly, the following guidelines can help you manage your time within each section:

DID YOU KNOW?

Some students find it helpful to make a list or spreadsheet of the different factors that make various answer choices incorrect.

Aim to complete the first ten Logical Reasoning questions within ten minutes. This will give you twenty-five minutes to complete the remaining problems. Additionally, you might find it helpful to pause for fifteen to thirty seconds at the end of question 10. Go back and review your answers, circle any that you might wish to come back to, and bubble in your answer sheet.

An alternative bubbling strategy is to bubble your answers at the end of every two pages before you turn to the next set of two pages. This gives you ten to fifteen seconds to clear your mind before moving on to the next set. Although the LSAT is a time-pressured test, do not be afraid to take short (less than one minute) breaks to rest your brain and ultimately improve your performance.

A Note About EXCEPT Questions

Several questions in each Logical Reasoning section will likely be EXCEPT questions, such as the following:

- Each of the following, if true, strengthens the argument EXCEPT…
- If all of the statements in the passage are true, each of the following must also be true EXCEPT…

The word *EXCEPT* will always be capitalized so that you do not overlook it. You might choose to underline or circle the EXCEPT to focus your mind.

Be careful with these questions. In the first example above, you should *not* assume that the correct answer will *weaken* the argument. The question is telling you that four of the five answers will strengthen the argument, and that one will not. It is not saying that the right answer will weaken the argument—it might simply not add anything at all, or it might be completely irrelevant.

The best approach is to simply find and eliminate the four answers that actually do strengthen the argument. Whatever remains is the right answer.

The same logic applies to the second example above. Do not look for an answer that *must* be false. Instead, eliminate those four answer choices that *must* be true. Your correct answer is one that *could* be false, not one that *must* be false.

Passage-Based Questions

This family of questions tests your ability to read a short passage and identify what the author is saying or arguing. These questions ask you to assess *only* the author's statements and any reasonable assumptions they require, or any inferences that follow from the statements.

The diagram accompanying this family (see Table 3.3) shows an arrow pointing from the passage to the answers. This represents the idea that your answer choice comes directly out of the passage. In the pages that follow, each of the seven Passage-Based questions will be discussed in greater detail. Generally, these questions are simple to understand, although they may be very difficult to solve. They gauge your ability to use deductive reasoning to choose an answer that either restates part of the passage or follows from the passage as a logical consequence.

TABLE 3.3. Passage-Based Questions

QUESTION TYPES	GENERAL STRATEGIES	FAMILY DIAGRAM
1. Main Conclusion 2. Inference (Must Be True/Must Be False) 3. Inference (Most Strongly Supported) 4. Necessary Assumption 5. Point at Issue 6. Underlying Principle 7. Principle Application	1. Your answer comes from the passage, so stick to the facts. 2. Ignore outside information. 3. Watch for extreme language.	**Passage** Answers

Main Conclusion Questions

These questions use key phrases and words like *main point* and *conclusion.* Questions may include:

- Which one of the following most accurately expresses the main conclusion of the argument?

- Which one of the following most accurately restates the main point of the passage?

- Which one of the following most logically completes the argument?

When reading these passages, put yourself in the author's shoes. Read the passage as though you were really *arguing* with someone—not just reciting words on a page. Then, if you had just one clause to make your point, what would you say?

Practice articulating conclusions in this way as you work through Logical Reasoning questions. You may notice yourself using words like *because* or *since* in your paraphrased conclusions. Try to avoid those words. As soon as you say *because*, you have left conclusion territory to state a premise. Your task is to isolate the conclusion of the argument as separate from the premises.

Review common patterns of reasoning, including the "Some people think [*x* is true], but…" pattern, cause and effect, argument by analogy, advocacy, and prediction. Also review the concepts of premise and conclusion.

SPECIFIC TIPS FOR MUST BE TRUE/MUST BE FALSE QUESTIONS

1. Separate the conclusion from the premises.

2. The answer will not be a summary of the whole passage. It should just be a paraphrase of the clause of the sentence that is the author's conclusion.

3. When you see the "Some people think [*x* is true], but…"pattern of reasoning, the conclusion is "*x* is false."

Look for the clause or sentence that is the author's conclusion, and expect the answer to restate it. In questions that ask you to fill in the blank by completing an unfinished passage, come up with a conclusion that is safely supported by all the facts presented.

Look for conclusion indicators like *thus*, *therefore*, *so*, *consequently*, and *hence*. Additionally, look for words like *probably*, *must have*, and *should*, which are often found in conclusion sentences even in the absence of a conclusion indicator.

COMMON MISCONCEPTIONS

1. You do not need to summarize the entire passage; a single line or clause is sufficient.

2. The fact that the answer is stated in the passage does not automatically make it correct. It might well be a premise, in which case it is *true*, but incorrect.

★ LSAT EXAM QUESTION

10.1.11.

The fire that destroyed the Municipal Building started before dawn this morning, and the last firefighters did not leave until late this afternoon. No one could have been anywhere in the vicinity of a fire like that one and fail to notice it. Thomas must have seen it, whatever he now says to the contrary. He admits that, as usual, he went from his apartment to the library this morning, and there is no way for him to get from his apartment to the library without going past the Municipal Building.

1. The main conclusion of the argument is that

   A) Thomas was in the vicinity of the fire this morning.

   B) Thomas claimed not to have seen the fire.

   C) Thomas saw the fire this morning.

   D) Thomas went directly from his apartment to the library this morning.

   E) Thomas went by the Municipal Building this morning.

Inference (Must Be True/Must Be False) Questions

Must Be True questions feature key phrases and words like *must be true*, *drawn from the passage*, *inferred*, *properly concluded*, *follows logically*, and *inference*. Questions may resemble the following:

- Which one of the following conclusions can be properly drawn from the statements above?

- Which one of the following can be properly inferred from Dr. Z's statement?

- If the statements above are true, which one of the following must be true?

To identify Must Be False questions, keep an eye out for key phrases and words like *cannot be true*, *inconsistent*, *conflicts with*, and *could be true, EXCEPT*. Must Be False questions may look like the following:

- Those whose view is described are able to hold inconsistent beliefs if they also believe that...

- If the statements in the passage are true, each of the following could be true EXCEPT...

- If the statements above are true, then which one of the following must be false?

Read the passage as a plain set of facts, rather than as an argument. Do not worry about distinguishing premises and conclusions here. Your job is to consider each proposition as a true fact and to discover what else must be true or false based on the facts stated.

These can be the hardest questions for which to anticipate an answer, because many plausible inferences can arise from a set of facts. However, look for conditional statements and seek to make inferences from them. Frequently when conditional statements are in the passage, the answer is an inference that follows from those statements. Master the common patterns of deductive reasoning so that you can distinguish between valid and invalid inferences.

SPECIFIC TIPS FOR MUST BE TRUE/MUST BE FALSE QUESTIONS

1. The answer does not need to summarize the passage.

2. Do not worry about conclusions here. Treat the entire passage (and all its implications) as factual truth.

3. The answer can paraphrase (or contradict) any single fact or clause of the passage, even in a long and convoluted passage.

4. Must Be True: The answer must come directly from the facts. Prefer safe language over extreme language.

5. Must Be False: The answer must directly contradict the facts.

COMMON MISCONCEPTIONS

1. You do not need to summarize or refute the entire passage.

2. You are not looking for the author's main point, so a single fact from the passage is sufficient.

3. You should not have normative language in your answer unless there is normative language in the passage.

★ LSAT EXAM QUESTION
Inference—Must Be True
1.1.14.

Historically, monetary systems have developed only in population centers with marketplaces. Through the fourth century BC, Mesopotamian cities engaged in trade but had never had marketplaces. By that period, however, Greek cities all had marketplaces, or *agorae*. The Greek cities' agorae were centrally located, and goods were traded there either for money or for commodities.

2. If all the statements in the passage are true, then which one of the following must also be true?

   A) In the fourth century BC, Greek cities were the only population centers with monetary systems.

   B) The development of monetary systems has historically led to the development of marketplaces.

   C) In the fourth century BC, the Greeks and the Mesopotamians traded with each other.

   D) After the fourth century BC, Mesopotamian cities had marketplaces and monetary systems.

   E) The Mesopotamian cities of the fourth century BC did not have monetary systems.

★ **LSAT EXAM QUESTION**
Inference—Must Be False
2.1.17.

The advanced technology of ski boots and bindings has brought a dramatic drop in the incidence of injuries that occur on the slopes of ski resorts: from nine injuries per one thousand skiers in 1950 to three in 1980. As a result, the remainder of ski-related injuries, which includes all injuries occurring on the premises of a ski resort but not on the slopes, rose from 10 percent of all ski-related injuries in 1950 to 25 percent in 1980. The incidence of these injuries, including accidents such as falling down steps, increases with the amount of alcohol consumed per skier.

3. Which of the following conflicts with information in the passage?

   A) The number of ski injuries that occurred on the slopes was greater in 1980 than in 1950.

   B) A skier was less likely to be injured on the slopes in 1950 than in 1980.

   C) The reporting of ski injuries became more accurate between 1950 and 1980.

   D) The total number of skiers dropped between 1950 and 1980.

   E) Some ski-related injuries occurred in 1980 to people who were not skiing.

Inference (Most Strongly Supported) Questions

These questions contain straightforward key phrases like *most strongly supported (by the passage)*. Some examples include:

- The statements above, if true, give the most support to which one of the following?
- The passage provides the most support for which one of the following?
- If the statements above are true, which one of the following conclusions is most strongly supported by them?

Most Strongly Supported, or Inference, questions are similar to Must Be True questions. Read the passage as a bare set of facts rather than as an argument, even if the author has premises and a conclusion.

Many times, the answer to a Most Strongly Supported question will be an answer that must be true. That is, answer these questions the way you would respond to a Must Be True question.

Therefore, the same advice applies. When you see conditional statements, make inferences and anticipate a possible answer that follows deductively from the conditional statements in the passage. If the passage has no conditional statements, it can be difficult to anticipate an answer. Just do your best to think through the logical consequences of the facts presented.

Unlike Must Be True questions, the answers to Most Strongly Supported questions can have some wiggle room: The answer might not be a statement that follows conclusively from the passage. Instead, you may need to pick an answer which, if it were the conclusion of an argument that took the passage as its premises, would produce at least a reasonably strong argument. Only one of the five answer choices will plausibly do this.

SPECIFIC TIPS FOR MOST STRONGLY SUPPORTED QUESTIONS

1. The answer should be almost certainly based on the passage.
2. Do not worry about conclusions here. Treat the entire passage (and all its implications) as factual truth.
3. Look first for an answer that absolutely must be true. If you do not see one, then choose the answer that, based on inductive reasoning, is very likely to be true.

AS WITH MUST BE TRUE/MUST BE FALSE QUESTIONS, IN INFERENCE QUESTIONS:

1. You do not need to summarize or refute the entire passage.
2. You are not looking for the author's main point, so just a single fact from the passage is sufficient.
3. You should not have normative language in your answer unless there is normative language in the passage.

HELPFUL HINT

Do not confuse a Most Strongly Supported question with a Strengthen question. Most Strongly Supported questions ask you which answer is supported by the passage. Strengthen questions, however, ask you which answer would *hypothetically* support the passage.

★ LSAT EXAM QUESTION

1.1.20.

Most people in the United States view neither big nor small business as particularly efficient or dynamic and regard both as providing consumers with fairly priced goods and services. However, most people consistently perceive small business as a force for good in society, whereas big business is perceived as socially responsible only in terms of prosperity.

4. The statements above, if true, would provide the strongest support for which one of the following hypotheses?

   A) Most people in the United States give little thought to the value of business to society.

   B) If big business were more efficient, it would be perceived more favorably by the public generally.

C) If small business were regarded as being more dynamic, it, too would receive strongly favorable ratings only in times of general prosperity.

D) Even if people did not regard big business as providing consumers with value for their money, they would still regard it as socially responsible in times of general prosperity.

E) Many people in the United States regard the social responsibility of big business as extending beyond providing consumers with fairly priced goods and services.

Necessary Assumption Questions

Necessary Assumption questions feature key words and phrases like *assumes*, *presupposes*, *required assumption*, and *depends on*. Questions might look like this:

- The argument assumes which one of the following?

- Which one of the following is an assumption upon which the argument in the passage depends?

- The argument presupposes that which one of the following assumptions is required by the argument?

When reading Necessary Assumption questions, look for two things:

1. holes in the argument

2. possible objections to the argument

Holes in the argument are actual gaps between the language of the premises and the language of the conclusion. For example, analyze this assertion: "Europeans have a lower risk of heart disease than North Americans. Therefore, Europeans are healthier than North Americans."

Here, there is a gap between "lower risk of heart disease" and "healthier." The author must be assuming that "no factors other than risk of heart disease affect the relative health of Europeans and North Americans."

Arguments like this commit the fallacy of missing the point; many Necessary Assumption questions commit this fallacy. Your job is to identify how the author is "jumping to conclusions" and articulate what the author must believe in order for the stated premises to actually support the stated conclusion.

Even in arguments that do not have clear disconnections between the premises and the conclusion, look for potential weaknesses, also known as **possible objections to the argument**. An author must necessarily assume that any potential weakeners are false. Thus, you can identify a necessary assumption by finding an answer that rules out a potential weakener.

For example, consider this: "Laura drives a blue Ford Focus and gets twenty-five miles per gallon. A car's make and model tend to indicate its gas mileage. Therefore, if Jordan buys a blue Ford Focus, he will also get twenty-five miles per gallon."

Here, there is no obvious gap between the language of the premises and the language of the conclusion. But is this a perfect argument? No. All we know is that make and model *tend to* indicate gas mileage; we do not know that they *guarantee* identical gas mileage.

Possible objections might therefore be "What if Jordan uses a lot more air conditioning than Laura?" or "What if Laura drives on country roads, and Jordan drives only in city traffic?" Surely, if the author thought these objections were true, he would not be able to make the original argument. That's why the author must *necessarily* assume that these potential weakeners are false in order for the argument to be plausible.

Possible Necessary Assumption answer choices here could be "It is not the case that Jordan uses a lot more air conditioning than Laura," or "Jordan's highway-to-city driving ratio is not substantially lower than Laura's."

When answering Necessary Assumption questions, keep the following in mind:

- If you notice a "hole" or language gap, anticipate an answer that connects the premises to the conclusion using safe language.

- Consider possible objections to the argument and construct an assumption that defends the argument against those possible objections, especially in cause-and-effect arguments.
  - If the author is arguing based on a correlation between x and y that x is the cause of y, then the author must necessarily assume that y is not the cause of x and there is no third factor that causes both x and y.
  - Adding either of these two statements as a necessary assumption defends the causal conclusion against alternate possible conclusions.

SPECIFIC TIPS FOR NECESSARY ASSUMPTION QUESTIONS

1. The answer is something the author must absolutely believe to be true in order to make the argument. If the correct answer were *false*, then the argument would be destroyed.

2. Be careful not to assume the answer along with the passage. In many cases, the necessary assumption is so obvious that the reader simply assumes that the author has stated it. Remember, a necessary assumption is an unstated premise in an argument.

3. The answer must be true based on the passage. Treat these questions as Inference/Must Be True questions.

THE NEGATION TEST

Use the negation test to confirm that your selected answer is indeed a necessary assumption:

> If you negate the correct answer and add it into the passage, it will destroy the argument.

This test holds true on every necessary assumption question. It can be time-consuming to negate lengthy answer choices and evaluate how they would affect the passage, so do not apply the negation test to every answer choice. Rather, once you have settled on one or two answers that could be correct, use the negation test to confirm that your answer is necessary.

Here's how the negation test works. A necessary assumption is defined as a premise that the author must believe to be true in order for the argument to be sound.

We could state this as a conditional statement: "If the argument is sound, then the necessary assumption must be true."

The negation test is the contrapositive of the above statement: "If a necessary assumption is false, then the argument will not be sound."

This means that four of the answer choices could be negated while still being fully consistent with the argument in the passage. However, the correct answer's negated form is inconsistent with the argument in the passage. That's why the correct answer, in its positive (non-negated) form, is an assumption required by the argument.

COMMON MISCONCEPTIONS

1. The correct answer does not need to justify the conclusion. There may be many (even infinite) necessary assumptions in a given argument, but your job is simply to identify one necessary assumption.

    Consider this example: All adult male citizens of Athens could vote. Therefore, Socrates could vote.

    Here, a valid answer would be "Socrates was male." Another answer would be "Socrates was a citizen of Athens." Another answer would be "Socrates attained adulthood." You *could* get an answer like "Socrates was an adult male citizen of Athens," and this would be correct, but that type of answer (which is both a necessary assumption and a sufficient assumption) is not required.

2. Language that appears "outside the scope" of the argument may be exactly what you want in the right answer.

    In the earlier Ford Focus argument, for example, a valid answer could be "It is not the case that Jordan drives only on three-lane roads, which are notoriously bad for fuel economy." You might see the bit about three-lane roads as beyond the scope of the argument, but it is not: the answer is ruling out a potential weakener. How? If it *were* the case that Jordan drives only on three-lane roads that are notoriously bad for fuel economy, then it would certainly weaken the argument that Jordan will get twenty-five miles per gallon. The answer choice negates this potential weakener and is therefore a necessary assumption.

1.1.19.

Train service suffers when a railroad combines commuter and freight service. By dividing its attention between its freight and commuter customers, a railroad serves neither particularly well. Therefore, if a railroad is going to be a successful business, then it must concentrate exclusively on one of these two markets.

5. For the argument to be logically correct, it must make which one of the following assumptions?

    A) Commuter and freight service have little in common with each other.

    B) The first priority of a railroad is to be a successful business.

    C) Unless a railroad serves its customers well, it will not be a successful business.

    D) If a railroad concentrates on commuter service, it will be a successful business.

    E) Railroad commuters rarely want freight service as well.

Point at Issue Questions

Point at Issue questions feature key phrases and words like *point at issue*, *disagree*, and *committed to disagreeing*. Some examples include the following:

- The point at issue between Jones and Smith is...

- On the basis of their statements, Shanna and Jorge are committed to disagreeing about the truth of which one of the following statements?

- The dialogue most supports the claim that Tony and Raoul disagree about whether...

Passages accompanying Point at Issue questions always feature two speakers or authors. Identify each speaker's conclusion. Sometimes, the point of disagreement will be the speaker's conclusions. Other times, the speakers might agree with each other's conclusions but disagree with a premise or assumption.

To answer Point at Issue questions, think of a complete sentence for which one of the speakers must say, "Yes, that's true," and the other speaker must say, "No, that's false." This can simply be a clause or sentence taken from either one of the speaker's arguments.

SPECIFIC TIPS FOR POINT AT ISSUE QUESTIONS

1. Apply the **yes-no test**. For your answer, one of the two speakers must be committed to saying, "Yes, that is true," and the other must be committed to saying, "No that is false."

2. If there is any possible way for the two speakers to agree that the answer is true *or* that the answer is false, it is a wrong answer.

COMMON MISCONCEPTIONS

The answer can restate a premise or a conclusion directly from *one* of the speaker's arguments. Even if the other speaker does not directly negate that proposition, the answer is correct if the other speaker would be committed to disagreeing with the proposition based on what is stated.

2.2.13.

Alia: Hawthorne admits that he has influence with high government officials. He further admits that he sold that influence to an environmental interest group. There can be no justification for this kind of unethical behavior.

Martha: I disagree that he was unethical. The group that retained Hawthorne's services is dedicated to the cause of preventing water pollution. So, in using his influence to benefit this group, Hawthorne also benefited the public.

6. Alia and Martha disagree on whether

    A) the meaning of ethical behavior has changed over time.

    B) the consequences of Hawthorne's behavior can ethically justify that behavior.

    C) the standards for judging ethical behavior can be imposed on Hawthorne by another.

    D) the meaning of ethical behavior is the same in a public situation as in a private one.

    E) the definition of ethical behavior is rooted in philosophy or religion.

Underlying Principle Questions

To identify Underlying Principle questions, keep an eye out for key words and phrases along the lines of *the argument appeals to/is based on/conforms to/expresses a principle*. Questions may read as follows:

- The argument tacitly appeals to which one of the following principles?

- The physician's reasoning could be based on which one of the following principles?

- The reasoning in the argument most closely conforms to which one of the following principles?

- Which one of the following expresses a general principle that could underlie the argument?

As you read the passage, think, "What is this passage an example of?" For example, consider this argument: "Bob had four weeks to make the PowerPoint presentation that he was assigned to complete by this afternoon. The topic was simple, and he could have asked us questions if he didn't know how to proceed. His email this morning telling us that the presentation was beyond his ability and that he would not be able to complete it is therefore inexcusable, and he should be sanctioned." The underlying principle here could be "Failure to complete a task for which one has ample time to seek help is inexcusable and worthy of sanctions." This is a general principle, which could broadly apply to any number of situations, of which the preceding passage is one possible situation.

To answer Underlying Principle questions, generalize from the subject matter detail of the passage to a broader, more generic statement. In the preceding example, step back from PowerPoint and emails, and craft a broader statement that applies to the passage and can also apply to other analogous situations.

SPECIFIC TIPS FOR UNDERLYING PRINCIPLE QUESTIONS

1. Your answer should be a general principle that could guide the author's reasoning. Often, it is a principle that could serve to connect the argument's premises with its conclusion.

2. The passage should be an example of your chosen answer.

COMMON MISCONCEPTIONS

The correct answer does not need to mention any specifics from the passage. It can be very vague, broad, murky, and poorly worded.

★ LSAT EXAM QUESTION

2.2.1.

A major art theft from a museum was remarkable in that the pieces stolen clearly had been carefully selected. The criterion for selection, however, clearly had not been the greatest estimated market value. It follows that the theft was specifically carried out to suit the taste of some individual collector for whose private collection the pieces were destined.

7. The argument tacitly appeals to which one of the following principles?

A) Any art theft can, on the evidence of the selection of pieces stolen, be categorized as committed either at the direction of a single known individual or at the direction of a group of known individuals.

B) Any art theft committed at the direction of a single individual results in a pattern of works taken and works left alone that defies rational analysis.

C) The pattern of works taken and works left alone can sometimes distinguish one type of art theft from another.

D) Art theft committed with no preexisting plan for the disposition of the stolen works does not always involve theft of only the most valuable pieces.

E) The pattern of works taken and works left alone in an art theft can be particularly damaging to the integrity of the remaining collection.

Principle Application Questions

Principle Application questions often feature this phrase: *Judgment below conforms to the principle above.* Principle Application questions may read as follows:

- Which one of the following judgments conforms to the principle stated above?

- Which one of the following judgments most closely conforms to the principle cited above?

Here, the passage is a principle, and the answer will be an example of the passage. Compare that to underlying principle questions, where the answer is a principle and the passage is an example of the answer. Very frequently, you will see conditional statements in the passage. Diagram them.

If you have a conditional statement in the form "If A is true then B is true," expect the answer's conclusion to be "A is false or B is true."

SPECIFIC TIPS FOR PRINCIPLE APPLICATION QUESTIONS

1. Here, the passage is the principle, and the answer is an example of the principle.

2. Diagram conditional statements.

3. Do not confuse "if" statements with "only if" statements.

4. A principle in the form "If A is true then B is true" can never support the conclusion that A is true or that B is false. It can only support a conclusion that B is true (because A is true) or a conclusion that A is false (because B is false).

COMMON MISCONCEPTIONS

Your answer does not need to be an example of the *entire* passage; it can be an example of just one sentence or conditional statement from the passage, so long as it remains *consistent* with the whole passage.

★ LSAT EXAM QUESTION

3.2.24.

It has been claimed that an action is morally good only if it benefits another person and was performed with that intention, whereas an action that harms another person is morally bad either if such harm was intended or if reasonable forethought would have shown that the action was likely to cause harm.

8. Which one of the following judgments most closely conforms to the principle cited above?

    A) Pamela wrote a letter attempting to cause trouble between Edward and his friend; this action of Pamela's was morally bad, even though the letter, in fact, had an effect directly opposite from the one intended.

    B) In order to secure a promotion, Jeffrey devoted his own time to resolving a backlog of medical benefits claims; Jeffrey's action was morally good since it alone enabled Sara's claim to be processed in time for her to receive much needed treatment.

    C) Intending to help her elderly neighbor by clearing his walkway after a snowstorm, Teresa inadvertently left ice on his steps; because of this exposed ice, her neighbor had a bad fall, thus showing that morally good actions can have bad consequences.

    D) Marilees, asked by a homeless man for food, gave the man her own sandwich; however, because the man tried to talk while he was eating the sandwich, it caused him to choke, and thus Marilees unintentionally performed a morally bad action.

    E) Jonathan agreed to watch his three-year-old niece while she played but, becoming engrossed in conversation, did not see her run into the street where she was hit by a bicycle; even though he intended no harm, Jonathan's action was morally bad.

Hypothetical Questions

This family of questions tests your ability to read a short passage and bring in new information to answer the question asked. Hypothetical questions include variations of these question stems:

Which of the following, *if true* (or, *if assumed*), would

- *strengthen* the reasoning above?
- *weaken* the reasoning above?
- *justify* the conclusion above?
- *resolve* the apparent paradox above?

TABLE 3.4. Hypothetical Questions		
QUESTION TYPES	**GENERAL STRATEGIES**	**FAMILY DIAGRAM**
1. Strengthen 2. Weaken 3. Justify ("Sufficient Assumption") 4. Resolve	1. You are adding an answer choice into the argument in order to answer the question. 2. Extreme language can be ideal. 3. Never eliminate an answer because "it isn't true" — the question told you to assume that all of the answer choices are true!	Passage Answers

GENERAL TIPS FOR HYPOTHETICAL QUESTIONS

1. You are bringing in new information (a new premise, if the passage is an argument) to answer the question.

2. Extreme language can be ideal.

3. Never eliminate an answer because "it isn't true." The question says to assume that all the answer choices are true.

★ LSAT EXAM QUESTION

30.2.20

Consumer advocate: The introduction of a new drug into the marketplace should be contingent upon our having a good understanding of its social impact. However, the social impact of the newly marketed antihistamine is far from clear. It is obvious, then, that there should be a general reduction in the pace of bringing to the marketplace new drugs that are now being tested.

9. Which one of the following, if true, most strengthens the argument?

   A) The social impact of the new antihistamine is much better understood than that of most new drugs being tested.

B) The social impact of some of the new drugs being tested is poorly understood.

C) The economic success of some drugs is inversely proportional to how well we understand their social impact.

D) The new antihistamine is chemically similar to some of the new drugs being tested.

E) The new antihistamine should be on the market only if most new drugs being tested should be on the market.

Strengthen Questions

To identify Strengthen questions, look for key words and phrases like *supports*, *strengthens*, *bolsters*, and *provides the strongest evidence for*. Questions might look like this:

- Which one of the following, if true, would most strengthen the argument?

- Which one of the following, if true, supports the conclusion in the passage?

- Which one of the following, if true, most strongly supports the explanation given in the argument?

When reading the passage, your primary goal is to identify the conclusion. Put yourself in the author's shoes and think about what other evidence you would like to have to make your conclusion more likely.

When answering Strengthen questions, stop and think about possible factors that would strengthen the argument if true. Do not confine yourself to the factors discussed in the premises: anything that would make the conclusion more likely is a strengthener.

SPECIFIC TIPS FOR STRENGTHEN QUESTIONS

1. Rule out an alternate possible cause of an effect to strengthen a cause-and-effect argument.

2. Anything that strengthens the conclusion is fair game, even if it seems to go beyond the scope of the stated premises.

3. The answer choices cannot negate a premise of the argument. If an answer appears to negate (and thus apparently weaken) the argument, stop to see how the answer might work with the premises of the argument to produce a strengthening inference.

COMMON MISCONCEPTIONS

As discussed above, an answer choice cannot actually negate a premise of an argument. Look for answer choices that appear to be contradicting a premise of the argument but are actually narrowing the scope of the premise in a way that strengthens the argument.

Look for assumptions. An answer choice that states (thereby validating) an assumption by affirming that the assumption is true closes up a possible hole in the argument.

For cause-and-effect arguments, anticipate an answer that rules out an alternate possible cause of the effect as explained by the argument. (See "Condition, Correlation, and Causation" in Chapter 1.)

Do not confuse a Most Strongly Supported question with a Strengthen question.

- Most Strongly Supported questions ask which answer is supported by the passage.
- Strengthen questions ask which answer would hypothetically support the passage.
- The words *most strongly support* can appear in *either* type of question, so pay attention to whether the passage is supporting the answer or the answer is supporting the passage.

★ LSAT EXAM QUESTION

7.2.1.

In 1974 the speed limit on highways in the United States was reduced to fifty-five miles per hour in order to save fuel. In the first twelve months after the change, the rate of highway fatalities dropped 15 percent, the sharpest one-year drop in history. Over the next ten years, the fatality rate declined by another 2 percent. It follows that the 1974 reduction in the speed limit saved many lives.

10. Which one of the following, if true, most strengthens the argument?

A) The 1974 fuel shortage cut driving sharply for more than a year.

B) There was no decline in the rate of highway fatalities during the twelfth year following the reduction in the speed limit.

C) Since 1974, automobile manufacturers have been required by law to install lifesaving equipment, such as seatbelts, in all new cars.

D) The fatality rate in highway accidents involving motorists driving faster than fifty-five miles per hour is much higher than in highway accidents that do not involve motorists driving at such speeds.

E) Motorists are more likely to avoid accidents by matching their speed to that of the surrounding highway traffic than by driving at faster or slower speeds.

Weaken Questions

To identify Weaken questions, look out for key words and phrases like *undermine, weaken, call into question,* and *cast doubt upon*. Some examples of Weaken questions follow:

- Which one of the following, if true, would best challenge the conclusion of the passage?
- Which one of the following, if true, most seriously weakens the argument?

- Which one of the following, if true, casts the most doubt on the author's hypothesis?

- Which one of the following, if true, most undermines the conclusion above?

When reading the passage, be critical. First identify the conclusion, then look at and identify why the premises do not support the conclusion. Look for possible fallacies. Raise objections to the argument as you read.

To answer these questions, first state the counterargument by negating the conclusion. Then anticipate an answer that strengthens the counterargument. Additionally, in cause-and-effect arguments, the answer often presents an alternate possible cause of an effect that the argument is trying to explain. Finally, think about the author's assumptions, and anticipate an answer that negates an assumption in order to weaken the passage. (See "Weakening Assumptions," on the next page.)

SPECIFIC TIPS FOR WEAKEN QUESTIONS

1. Bring in an alternate possible cause of an effect to weaken a cause-and-effect argument.

2. Anything that weakens the conclusion is fair game, even if seems to go beyond the scope of the stated premises.

3. Weaken the argument by either (1) presenting an alternative conclusion or (2) weakening the logical connection between the stated premise(s) and the conclusion.

COMMON MISCONCEPTIONS

As previously discussed, an answer choice cannot negate an argument's premise. Accordingly, you will never have an answer choice that weakens an argument simply by contradicting a premise that has already been stated. Consider this example:

Politician: Pollution in North Dakota is now higher than it has ever been in recorded history. If we do not take action to curb pollution emissions in North Dakota, it will not be long before our citizens begin to suffer grave health-related consequences. Therefore, the new proposal to cap pollution at pre-2005 levels must be adopted.

Here, you will never have an answer choice that says something like "Pollution in North Dakota is actually at its lowest point in recorded history" because all of the premises of the argument remain in full effect as you apply the answer choices. This is what we mean when we say an answer will never negate a premise of the argument. Your goal in weakening the argument is to make the conclusion less likely. You can do this either by affirming an alternative conclusion or by weakening the logical connection between the premise and the conclusion. Here are two possible weakeners for this argument:

1. An alternate proposal to work with neighboring states to reduce their pollution would be more effective in preventing pollution-related health disorders in North Dakota.

This weakens the argument by presenting an alternate conclusion. If this is true (and remember, the question tells you to assume it is true), then this undermines the argument's conclusion that the pre-2005 proposal should be adopted.

> 2. North Dakota has the lowest pollution rate in the country, and even citizens of the states with the highest pollution rates have not experienced any health-related consequences because of pollution.

This weakens the argument by weakening the logical connection between the premise and the conclusion. Notice that this answer choice does not actually negate the premise of the argument. It is not contradicting the statement that pollution in North Dakota is higher than ever. Rather, if this answer is true (and remember, the question says to assume it is true), it shows that the pollution in North Dakota is not really a problem. Although pollution is higher than ever, it is still relatively low, and there is no cause for concern over the health issues mentioned by the politician.

WEAKENING ASSUMPTIONS

You can also think of the second weakener above as an attack against one of the author's implicit assumptions. In making the argument, the author's necessary assumption is "The fact that North Dakota's pollution is higher than ever is cause for health concern." By bringing in a sentence that effectively says, "No, it isn't," you negate the assumption, weakening the argument.

★ **LSAT EXAM QUESTION**

3.1.20.

In Brazil, side-by-side comparison of Africanized honeybees and the native honeybees has shown that the Africanized bees are far superior honey producers. Therefore, there is no reason to fear that domestic commercial honey production will decline in the United States if local honeybees are displaced by Africanized honeybees.

11. Each of the following, if true, would weaken the argument EXCEPT

A) the honeybees native to Brazil are not of the same variety as those most frequently used in the commercial beekeeping industry in the United States.

B) commercial honey production is far more complicated and expensive with Africanized honeybees than it is with the more docile honeybees common in the United States.

C) if Africanized honeybees replace local honeybees, certain types of ornamental trees will be less effectively pollenated.

D) in the United States a significant proportion of the commercial honey supply comes from hobby beekeepers, many of whom are likely to abandon beekeeping with the influx of Africanized bees.

E) the area of Brazil where the comparative study was done is far better suited to the foraging habits of the Africanized honeybees than are most areas of the United States.

★ **60.1.16.**

Company spokesperson: In lieu of redesigning our plants, our company recently launched an environmental protection campaign to buy and dispose of old cars, which are generally highly pollutive. Our plants account for just 4 percent of the local air pollution, while automobiles that predate 1980 account for 30 percent. Clearly, we will reduce air pollution more by buying old cars than we would be redesigning our plants.

12. Which one of the following, if true, most seriously weakens the company spokesperson's argument?

A) Only 1 percent of the automobiles driven in the local area predate 1980.

B) It would cost the company over $3 million to reduce its plants' toxic emissions, while its car-buying campaign will save the company money by providing it with reusable scrap metal.

C) Because the company pays only scrap metal prices for used cars, almost none of the cars sold to the company still run.

D) Automobiles made after 1980 account for over 30 percent of local air pollution.

E) Since the company launched its car-buying campaign, the number of citizen groups filing complaints about pollution from the company's plants has decreased.

Justify (Sufficient Assumption) Questions

To identify Justify questions, watch for key words and phrases like *if assumed*, *if valid*, *if established*, *would enable*, and *justify*. Questions may look like the following:

- The conclusion is properly drawn if which one of the following is assumed?

- Which one of the following is an assumption that would serve to justify the conclusion above?

- From which one of the following does the conclusion logically follow?

- Which one of the following is an assumption that would permit the conclusion above to be properly drawn?

- Which one of the following principles, if accepted, most strongly justifies drawing the conclusion above?

When reading the passage, first identify the conclusion and then discover why it is not fully supported by the premises. Think about completing this equation:

> Stated Premises + Your Sufficient Assumption =
> Fully Justified Conclusion

That is, you want to come up with a sentence that, combined with a premise (or premises) of the argument, would allow you to say, "Therefore, [conclusion]" with 100 percent logical certainty. Your goal is to justify the conclusion, turning the passage into a strong argument.

 DID YOU KNOW?

Don't confuse Sufficient Assumption with Necessary Assumption questions. Necessary Assumption questions ask what the author is assuming, whereas Sufficient Assumptions ask you to use outside assumptions to justify the passage. These questions require entirely different strategies.

Watch out for language that appears only in the conclusion. Your answer choice must fully justify the entire conclusion; it should usually include the same language as any new language in the conclusion. If you have a normative conclusion, for example, you must have a normative premise; if you don't, then the sufficient assumption must include normative language.

SPECIFIC TIPS FOR JUSTIFY/SUFFICIENT ASSUMPTION QUESTIONS

1. No matter how implausible or extreme, you want an answer that, if assumed, would make the argument airtight.

2. Read the conclusion of the argument; then say, "This has to be true because..."; and then read the premises and your selected answer. The conclusion of the argument should be inescapably valid based on the premises plus your chosen answer.

3. Sufficient assumptions are not actually assumptions. You are not identifying what the author is assuming. You are bringing in an extrinsic assumption to justify the author's reasoning.

COMMON MISCONCEPTIONS

1. Your answer needs to do more than strengthen the argument. It needs to completely connect the premises to the conclusion in a way that removes any possible "hole."

2. Your answer does not need to be reasonable. It can be something completely absurd, in ridiculously extreme language. The point is that if we assume the answer to be true, then the conclusion of the argument is inescapably true as well. (See Ford Focus argument in Part 2.)

★ **LSAT EXAM QUESTION**

3.2.17.

In a bureaucracy, all decisions are arrived at by a process that involves many people. There is no one person who has the authority to decide whether a project will proceed or not. As a consequence, in bureaucracies, risky projects are never undertaken.

13. The conclusion follows logically from the premises if which one of the following is assumed?

    A) All projects in a bureaucracy require risk.

    B) Decisive individuals choose not to work in a bureaucracy.

    C) An individual who has decision-making power will take risks.

    D) The only risky projects undertaken are those for which a single individual has decision-making power.

    E) People sometimes take risks as individuals that they would not take as part of a group.

Resolve Questions

To identify Resolve questions, look out for key words like *resolve*, *explain*, *reconcile*, *conflict*, *paradox*, and *discrepancy*. Resolve questions may read as follows:

- Which one of the following, if true, most helps to resolve the paradox?

- Which one of the following, if true, best reconciles the discrepancy described above?

- Which one of the following, if true, does most to explain the apparently paradoxical outcome?

When reading the passage, expect to find an apparent paradox (that is, a situation where you have two facts and it does not seem like both could be true at the same time). Do not worry about premises and conclusions here; in many cases, the passage that accompanies Resolve questions will be a fact set rather than an argument.

To answer these questions, identify the apparent paradox or discrepancy. Then consider what would cause the paradoxical situation to make sense. For example, "Saturated fat leads to heart disease. The French eat lots of butter, which is high in saturated fat, but have very low rates of heart disease." Possible answers might include "The French also eat lots of fish, which counteracts the negative effects of saturated fat," or "The degree to which saturated fat leads to heart disease is minimal compared to almost every other food present in the diets of people in countries with high rates of heart disease."

SPECIFIC TIPS FOR RESOLVE QUESTIONS

1. First, identify the apparent paradox.

2. Stop and think: What would cause this to make sense?

3. Remember, not all of these passages are arguments. Some are mere fact sets and will not have a conclusion.

COMMON MISCONCEPTIONS

Remember that you should assume the answer choices to be true. Never cross out an answer choice as wrong because it is either untrue in real life or unstated/not implied within the passage. The answer is, by nature, outside information that you are *bringing into* the passage to make things right.

★ LSAT EXAM QUESTION

1.2.17.

A recent survey of brand preferences showed that R Bar Beans are considered the best of all brands among all age groups, leading both Texas T Beans and Aunt Sally's Beans by a wide margin. However, the national sales figures show that Texas T and Aunt Sally's each sold many more cans of beans last year than did R Bar.

14. Each of the following would, by itself, help to resolve the apparent paradox described in the passage EXCEPT

A) Texas T Beans and Aunt Sally's Beans are each much less expensive than R Bar Beans.

B) some of the surveyed age groups showed more of a preference for R Bar Beans than did others.

C) the survey was carried out only in the small geographic area where R Bar distributes its beans, not nationwide.

D) most food stores refuse to carry R Bar Beans because the manufacturer demands that R Bar Beans be carried exclusively.

E) R Bar Beans were only introduced to the market three months prior to the calculation of sales figures, while Texas T Beans and Aunt Sally's Beans had been available for years.

Critical Reasoning Questions

This family of questions tests your ability to describe, using logical terms, how the author is making an argument (see "LSAT Logic Vocabulary" in Chapter 1). In Method of Reasoning questions, you describe a strategy the author uses to make the argument. In Role of a Statement questions, you describe the function of a particular clause or sentence, usually by describing it as a premise, conclusion, example, analogy, or intermediate conclusion. In Argument Flaw questions, you identify fallacies within the author's reasoning. In Evaluate the Argument questions, you assess what would be needed to determine whether the argument's conclusion is sound.

TABLE 3.5. Critical Reasoning Questions	
QUESTION TYPES	**GENERAL STRATEGIES**
1. Method of Reasoning	1. Focus on how the author argues, not what the author says.
2. Role of a Statement	
3. Argument Flaw	2. Paraphrase the structure of the argument as you read.
4. Evaluate the Argument	

GENERAL TIPS FOR CRITICAL REASONING QUESTIONS

1. Focus on how the author argues, not what the author says.

2. Paraphrase the structure of the argument as you read.

Method of Reasoning Questions

To identify Method of Reasoning questions, look for key phrases and words like *argumentative strategy* and *the author does*.

Sample wordings from actual LSAT tests include the following:

- In the passage, the author...

- In order to advance her point of view, the author does each of the following EXCEPT...

- The passage employs which one of the following argumentative strategies?
- Sims does which one of the following?

When reading the passage, identify the components of the argument: premise, intermediate conclusion, and conclusion. If any of the premises are examples or analogies, identify those as well. Do not worry about subject matter detail at all. In fact, it is best to paraphrase these passages as you read in a such way that omits subject matter detail entirely (see answer explanation below).

The correct answer is anything that describes something the author does within the argument. These questions are testing your ability to describe the structure of the argument, rather than its content.

SPECIFIC TIPS FOR METHOD OF REASONING QUESTIONS

1. Identify each component of the argument as you read. Look for premises, intermediate conclusions, and conclusions.

2. Be aware of examples and analogies.

3. Review "LSAT Logic Vocabulary" in Chapter 1.

AVOID COMMON MISCONCEPTIONS

No two answers will say the same thing. In these answer choices, every word is important. If you are about to choose an answer that says, "Presents evidence to refute a hypothesis," you should be able to identify the portion of the passage that matches up to evidence, and you should be able to identify a specific hypothesis refuted by the author. If any element of the answer choice is missing, then the answer is wrong.

★ LSAT EXAM QUESTION

2.2.3.

The United States has never been a great international trader. I found most of its raw material and customers for finished products within its own borders. The terrible consequences of this situation have become apparent, as this country now owes the largest foreign debt in the world and is a playground for wealthy foreign investors. The moral is clear: a country can no more live without foreign trade than a dog can live by eating its own tail.

15. In order to advance her point of view, the author does each of the following EXCEPT

A) draw on an analogy.

B) appeal to historical fact.

C) identify a cause and an effect.

D) suggest a cause of the current economic situation.

E) question the ethical basis of an economic situation.

Role of a Statement Questions

To identify Role of a Statement questions, look for key phrases and words like *plays which role* and *performs which function*. Role of Statement questions may look like the following:

- The phrase *certain traits like herding ability risk being lost among pedigreed dogs* serves which one of the following functions in the argument?

- The statement that adolescents and adults are not the same plays which one of the following roles in the argument?

The question will present a phrase or sentence from the passage and ask you to identify the phrase's function. Is it the argument's conclusion? Premise? Intermediate premise? Underline or bracket the phrase or sentence that the question is asking you about; that way, it stands out as you read the passage.

As you read the passage, identify the conclusion. If it matches the under-lined phrase or sentence, then your answer should be some variant of "It is the conclusion," such as "It is the claim that is supported by the remaining propo-sitions in the argument." If the phrase or sentence does not match the conclu-sion, then consider the premise and whether the phrase serves as an example or analogy. If it is not a premise, then is it just background information? If so, then it essentially plays no role in the argument other than to introduce the topic. Any of these functions are possible answers to the question. Ideally, you should be able to identify the role of the statement without looking at the answers. Spend your time on the passage, not the answers.

SPECIFIC TIPS FOR ROLE OF A STATEMENT QUESTIONS

1. Always stop and fully consider what role the statement plays before you even glance at the answer choices.

2. If the statement is simply a premise or a conclusion, then pick the answer that reflects that. Do not shy away from "easy" answers.

COMMON MISCONCEPTIONS

As with Method of Reasoning questions, no two answer choices will say the same thing, even if they look similar. Every word in the answer choice is important. Review the "LSAT Logic Vocabulary" in Chapter 1 and add any new words found in these answer choices to your vocabulary list, if you have trouble with them.

★ **LSAT EXAM QUESTION**

3.2.20.

Politician: Homelessness is a serious social problem, but further government spending to provide low-income housing is not the cure for homelessness. The most cursory glance at the real estate section of any major newspaper is enough to show that there is no lack of housing units available to rent. So the frequent claim that people are homeless because of a lack of available housing is wrong.

16. That homelessness is a serious social problem figures in the argument in which one of the following ways?

    A) It suggests an alternative perspective to the one adopted in the argument.

    B) It sets out a problem the argument is designed to resolve.

    C) It is compatible with either accepting the conclusion or denying it.

    D) It summarizes a position the argument as a whole is directed toward discrediting.

    E) It is required in order to establish the conclusion.

Argument Flaw Questions

To identify Argument Flaw questions, look for key words and phrases like *error in reasoning*, *vulnerable to criticism*, *weakness*, and *flaw*. Argument Flaw questions may look like the following:

- A major weakness of the argument is that it...

- A questionable technique used in the argument is to...

- A reasoning error in the argument is that the argument...

- The reasoning in the argument is not sound because it fails to establish that...

- Which one of the following describes a flaw in the argument?

When reading the passage, be critical. Identify the conclusion, then look at the premises and identify why the premises do not support the conclusion. Raise objections to the argument as you read.

Assuming you have thoroughly mastered the fallacies in Chapter 2 of this book, you should be able to identify the fallacy committed by the argument. Even if you do not call the fallacy by its name, you should be able to find a logical reason why the premises do not support the conclusion. Note that there are generally two forms in which the answers might be worded:

1. **Logical terms.** Sometimes the answers use wording similar to the actual definitions of the fallacies (like "draws a generalization on the basis of an unrepresentative sample").

2. **Factual terms.** Other times, the answers use wording heavily laden with the factual content of the passage (like "draws a generalization about all college students on the basis of a survey conducted at one college").

SPECIFIC TIPS FOR ARGUMENT FLAW QUESTIONS

1. Read the argument critically. Look for weaknesses.

2. Do not simply say, "That doesn't sound right." Finish the thought: "That doesn't sound right because [fallacy]."

3. Review the fallacies frequently to stay fresh.

COMMON MISCONCEPTIONS

Just because the answer choice describes a fallacy that the author *could have committed* does not make it the correct answer. Be sure that your answer describes something that the author is actually doing.

★ LSAT EXAM QUESTION

2.2.6.

Although this bottle is labeled "vinegar," no fizzing occurred when some of the liquid in it was added to powder from this box labeled "baking soda." But when an acidic liquid such as vinegar is added to baking soda, the resulting mixture fizzes, so this bottle clearly has been mislabeled.

17. A flaw in the reasoning in the argument above is that this argument

    A) ignores the possibility that the bottle contained an acidic liquid other than vinegar.

    B) fails to exclude an alternative explanation of the observed effect.

    C) depends on the use of the imprecise term *fizz*.

    D) does not take into account the fact that scientific principles can be definitely tested only under controlled laboratory conditions.

    E) assumes that the fact of a labeling error is proof of an intention to deceive.

Evaluate the Argument Questions

To identify Evaluate questions, look for key words and phrases like *evaluate* and *most helpful to know*. Evaluate questions may look as follows:

- Which one of the following would it be most useful to know in evaluating the argument?

- Clarification of which one of the following issues would be most important to an evaluation of the skeptic's position?

These questions are rare, appearing at a frequency of less than one question per LSAT. When reading the passage, identify uncertainties in the argument so that you can identify the kind of information that would help evaluate whether the conclusion is actually likely or not.

To answer these questions, pretend that you have been called upon to evaluate the conclusion's likelihood. You get to ask for additional information and additional premises. What extra information would you seek? Generally, the answers to these questions are themselves in the form of a question, so this is a good way of anticipating the answer.

Additionally, you need an answer that makes the conclusion strong or weak, depending on whether it is true or false. It would be useful to know if an answer has this sort of effect on the argument and would therefore be a good answer choice.

SPECIFIC TIPS FOR EVALUATE THE ARGUMENT QUESTIONS

    1. Read the argument very critically, in the same way that you would read the passage accompanying a Flaw question.

2. Answer choices usually start with "whether." As you read these choices, drop the "whether," and just read the rest of the answer. If the answer would strengthen the argument if it were true and weaken the argument if it were false (or vice versa), then it is exactly what you are looking for.

★ **LSAT EXAM QUESTION**

7.2.8.

George: Some scientists say that global warming will occur because people are releasing large amounts of carbon dioxide into the atmosphere by burning trees and fossil fuels. We can see, though, that the predicted warming is occurring already. In the middle of last winter, we had a month of spring-like weather in our area, and this fall, because of unusually mild temperatures, the leaves on our town's trees were three weeks late in turning color.

18. Which one of the following would be most relevant to investigate in evaluating the conclusion of George's argument?

   A) whether carbon dioxide is the only cause of global warming

   B) when leaves on the trees in the town usually change color

   C) what proportion of global emissions of carbon dioxide is due to the burning of trees by humans

   D) whether air pollution is causing some trees in the area to lose their leaves

   E) whether unusually warm weather is occurring elsewhere on the globe more frequently than before

Parallel Reasoning Questions

This family of questions, detailed in Table 3.6, tests your ability to isolate and match a pattern of reasoning, argument flaw, or underlying principle between two arguments. One of the skills that you will need as a law student and attorney is to be able to argue by analogy, and these questions test your ability to recognize when two arguments are actually analogous to each other. These questions tend to be long and time-consuming, but the concept of finding a matching argument is generally straightforward. The diagram accompanying this family shows a double-sided arrow, indicating that the passage will match an answer.

TABLE 3.6. Parallel Reasoning Questions

QUESTION TYPES	GENERAL STRATEGIES	FAMILY DIAGRAM
1. Parallel Pattern of Reasoning 2. Parallel Flaw 3. Parallel Principle	1. Identify the pattern of reasoning, argument flaw, or underlying principle of the passage as you read. 2. Match only the pattern of reasoning, not the content.	

GENERAL TIPS FOR PARALLEL REASONING QUESTIONS

1. Identify the pattern of reasoning, argument flaw, or underlying principle of the passage as you read.

2. Match only the pattern of reasoning, flaw, or principle, not the subject matter detail of the passage.

A NOTE ABOUT PARALLEL REASONING AND PARALLEL FLAW

Parallel Pattern of Reasoning questions are separated from Parallel Flaw questions because of the actual question that appears on the test. Sometimes it asks you to match the pattern of reasoning, and other times it asks you to match a flaw, indicating that the passage is flawed. However, even if it is a Parallel Pattern of Reasoning question, the argument might still be flawed. In such a case, you may be looking at a question that is effectively a Parallel Flaw question (that is, you will only have to match the flaw in an answer). Or, you may need to match more than just the flaw. Perhaps you will also need to match up extreme language in the conclusions, for example.

Parallel Pattern of Reasoning Questions

To identify Parallel Pattern of Reasoning questions, look for key words and phrases like *parallel*, *logical features*, *pattern of reasoning*, and *most similar*. Questions may be worded like the following:

- Which one of the following most closely parallels the reasoning used in the passage?

- Which one of the following has a logical structure most like that of the argument above?

- Which one of the following exhibits a pattern of reasoning that is most parallel to that used by the novelist?

Untangle the passage as you read: place the premises first, and then read the conclusion last. Diagram any conditional statements alongside the passage. If you have categorical statements, use Venn diagrams or concentric circles to diagram the premises only, and then see whether the conclusion is apparent from the premises. If it is, then the argument is valid; if it is not, the argument is flawed. Focus on the logical components of the passage.

To answer these questions, diagram the passage whenever possible, and preemptively think of an analogous argument. That way, when you read the correct answer, its similarity to the passage will stand out.

SPECIFIC TIPS FOR PARALLEL (PATTERN OF) REASONING QUESTIONS

1. Diagram conditional statements.

2. Do not confuse "if" statements with "only if" statements.

3. Use Venn diagrams or concentric circles to depict all/some/none statements.

COMMON MISCONCEPTIONS

Do not worry about the *order* of the sentences in the passage. This is *not* part of the structure of the argument, and it is not something that you have to match up in your answer. If the conclusion is first in the passage, it can be last in the correct answer.

★ LSAT EXAM QUESTION

1.1.6.

If Max were guilty, he would not ask the police to investigate. Therefore, his asking the police to investigate shows that he is not guilty.

19. The logical structure of the argument above is most similar to which one of the following?

   A) If Lucille were in the next room, I would not be able to see her. Therefore, the fact that I can see her shows that she is not in the next room.

   B) If Sam were rich, he would not spend his vacation in Alaska. Therefore, his spending his vacation in the Bahamas shows that he is rich.

   C) If Joe were over forty he would not want to learn to ski. Therefore, the fact that he does not want to learn to ski shows that he is over forty.

   D) If Mark were a good cook, he would not put cinnamon in the chili. Therefore, the fact that he is not a good cook shows that he put cinnamon in the chili.

   E) If Sally were sociable, she would not avoid her friends. Therefore, the fact that she is sociable shows that she does not avoid her friends.

Parallel Flaw Questions

To identify Parallel Flaw questions, look for key words and phrases like *similar flaw* and *similar error in reasoning*. Questions may resemble the following:

- Which one of the following contains an error of reasoning most similar to that made in the argument above?

- Which one of the following arguments contains a flaw that is most similar to one in the argument above?

These questions are *only* testing your ability to match the logical fallacy in the argument with the logical fallacy in the correct answer. Therefore, your primary focus when reading the passage should be to identify the fallacy.

Even if the passage is long and convoluted, the defining characteristic of the right answer is that it will contain the same fallacy as the passage. If the passage commits the fallacy of mistaken reversal, all a correct answer will need is mistaken reversal. Perhaps the answer will be similar in other regards (such as the number of premises or the order of the sentences), but this is not required.

SPECIFIC TIPS FOR PARALLEL ARGUMENT FLAW QUESTIONS

   1. Always stop at the end of the passage and determine the flaw.

   2. You only have to match the flaw. Even if the passage is long and convoluted, if the flaw is a simple mistaken reversal, you only need to find an answer with a mistaken reversal.

Many students try to take a shortcut by matching the language of the passage to the language of the answers. That is, they will see "always" or "should" in the passage and look for answers with similar wording. Do not do this! While it may sometimes work, it will sometimes cause you to eliminate the correct answer as well. Your job is to match the fallacy, not the wording of the argument.

★ LSAT EXAM QUESTION

2.2.22.

All intelligent people are nearsighted. I am very nearsighted. So I must be a genius.

20. Which one of the following exhibits both of the logical flaws exhibited in the argument above?

    A) I must be stupid because all intelligent people are nearsighted, and I have perfect eyesight.

    B) All chickens have beaks. This bird has a beak. So this bird must be a chicken.

    C) All pigs have four legs, but this spider has eight legs. So this spider must be twice as big as any pig.

    D) John is extremely happy, so he must be extremely tall, because all tall people are happy.

    E) All geniuses are very nearsighted. I must be very nearsighted, since I am a genius.

Parallel Principle Questions

To identify Parallel Principle questions, read the question carefully. In these questions, the passage and answers will all be arguments, without any principle explicitly stated in either the passage or the answers. Instead, the question itself will tell you that you are looking for an answer that is based on the same principle upon which the passage is based. Parallel Principle questions may look like this:

> Which one of the following most closely conforms to the principle that the passage above illustrates?

As you read the passage, think, "What is this passage an example of?" Come up with a general, broad principle for which the passage would be a good example, but which could also apply to a variety of other situations.

To answer these questions, come up with another situation to which your anticipated general principle could apply. This will help you spot the correct answer as you read the answer choices.

SPECIFIC TIPS FOR PARALLEL PRINCIPLE QUESTIONS

    1. These questions are the parallel version of Underlying Principle questions. Your job is to identify the principle that guides the author's reasoning in the original passage.

2. The principle is often a generalized form of "If premises like these are true, then a conclusion like this can follow."

3. The passage and your chosen answer should both be examples or illustrations of the same underlying principle.

COMMON MISCONCEPTIONS

You only have to match the underlying principle, not the argument's structure or language.

★ LSAT EXAM QUESTION

29.2.10.

Parents should not necessarily raise their children in the ways experts recommend, even if some of those experts are themselves parents. After all, parents are the ones who directly experience which methods are successful in raising their own children.

21. Which one of the following most closely conforms to the principle that the passage above illustrates?

   A) Although music theory is intrinsically interesting and may be helpful to certain musicians, it does not distinguish good music from bad: that is a matter of taste and not of theory.

   B) One need not pay much attention to the advice of automotive experts when buying a car if those experts are not interested in the mundane factors that concern the average consumer.

   C) In deciding the best way to proceed, a climber familiar with a mountain might do well to ignore the advice of mountain climbing experts unfamiliar with that mountain.

   D) A typical farmer is less likely to know what types of soil are most productive than is someone with an advanced degree in agricultural science.

   E) Unlike society, one's own conscience speaks with a single voice; it is better to follow the advice of one's own conscience than the advice of society.

Answer Key

Questions marked with a star are official LSAT questions provided by the LSAC.

★ **1.** **C) is correct.** Here, the author's conclusion is "Thomas must have seen it" (or, properly, "Thomas must have seen the fire"). Although containing no conclusion indicators, the passage does consist of many factual statements along with one "must have" statement indicating the author's opinion. You can state, "Thomas must have seen the fire," then ask, "Why?" The answer: "Because [all of the premises]." The stated premises jointly support the conclusion that Thomas saw the fire. Thus, while answers A) and E) are certainly *true* based on the passage, and while answer B) seems like a reasonable inference one might draw, these are not the author's conclusion. Answer D) is neither a premise nor a conclusion, as nothing says he went "directly" anywhere.

★ **2.** **E) is correct.** The correct answer must follow from the passage. Here, the first sentence is a conditional statement: "If monetary system, then marketplaces." The second sentence tells us that the Mesopotamians of the fourth century BC never had marketplaces. From this, we can logically infer (using the contrapositive pattern of deductive reasoning), that the Mesopotamians of the fourth century BC never had monetary systems. Answer A) does not work, for we cannot infer that *only* the Greeks had monetary systems. Answer B) is a general historical principle that is broader than anything we can conclude, and thus is incorrect. Answer C) does not work because there is no basis (according to the passage) to conclude that the Greeks and Mesopotamians even knew each other. Remember, do not refer to outside information—just stick to the facts of the passage. Finally, the passage does not contain any information about the Mesopotamians after the fourth century BC, so D) is not correct.

★ **3.** **B) is correct.** The correct answer must contradict the passage. Here, we know as a fact that nine out of one thousand skiers in 1950 were injured on the slopes, as opposed to three out of one thousand skiers in 1980. We do not know how many *total* skiers there were in either year, so we cannot draw any conclusions about the total number of ski injuries. Stating that the probability of on-slope injury was higher in 1980 than in 1950 contradicts what we know to be true from the passage. A) could be true if there were more than three times as many skiers in 1980 as in 1950, but we only know that the rate (or likelihood) of injury was lower in 1980 than in 1950. Nothing in the passage talks about reporting or the total number of skiers, so C) and D) are incorrect. E) is also incorrect because the passage states that 25 percent of ski-related injuries in 1980 were not on the slopes.

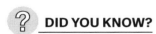

DID YOU KNOW?

Answers B) and C) in number 4 (LSAT example 1.1.20.) fall into the category of answer choices that are never correct. On Inference questions, you will never find a correct answer that makes a hypothetical prediction about a future condition, unless the passage specifically includes information that would justify such a prediction.

★ **4.** **E) is correct.** According to the passage, "most people in the United States" (1) do not see big businesses as efficient or dynamic, (2) think big business does provide fairly priced goods and services, and (3) see big business as socially responsible only during prosperous times. It can be inferred from this that big business must do something other than provide fairly priced goods and services for the public to view it as socially responsible. A) is incorrect. Nothing in the passage discusses how much thought people give to business in society. B) and C) are predictions. We have no way of knowing what would happen if big businesses were more efficient or if small businesses were regarded as more dynamic. D) is also incorrect. The passage does not say that people regard big businesses as socially responsible in times of prosperity. Rather, it says that people *only* regard big businesses as socially responsible in times of prosperity. This choice is therefore a mistaken reversal.

★ 5. **C) is correct.** Here, the premises tell us that if a railroad divides its attention between commuter and freight service, it will not serve its customers well. The conclusion tells us that if a railroad is a successful business, it does not divide its attention. This is the same as stating that if a railroad divides its attention, it will not be a successful business. The other four answers could all be false, and their negated forms would still be consistent with the argument. To make the argument, it is not necessary to assume that the other four statements are true, because the author could assume that they are false without compromising her logic. A) is incorrect because the two services *could* have a lot in common with each other. B) is incorrect because a railroad's first priority could be anything (e.g., safety). There is no reason to assume that being a successful business is a railroad's first priority. D) is incorrect because it is a sort of mistaken negation: the author must assume that if a railroad does *not* focus on a single service, it will *not* be successful, but the author does not have to assume that any railroad that *does* focus on a given service *will* be successful. This is extreme language. Concentrating on one service is required to be successful, but it does not ensure success. E) is incorrect because railroad commuters might *all* want freight service; there is no reason to assume that this statement is either true or false.

HELPFUL HINT

Read the question carefully; there have been a few LSAT questions that do not ask what the two speakers *disagree* about, but rather what they *agree* about. If you see such a question, choose an answer to which both speakers are either committed to saying, "That's true," or to saying, "That's false."

★ 6. **B) is correct.** Here, Alia's conclusion is that there is no justification for Hawthorne's unethical behavior of selling his political influence. Martha's conclusion is that Hawthorne's act of selling his political influence is not unethical. Martha's premise is that Hawthorne benefited the public by selling his influence, so her necessary assumption is "Selling political influence can be ethically justified if it benefits the public." Martha is committed to saying this sentence is true, while Alia is committed to saying it is false because she believes there cannot be any justification for Hawthorne's behavior.

★ 7. **C) is correct.** Here, the conclusion of the argument is that the art theft was conducted to acquire pieces for an individual collector. The premise is that the stolen pieces were carefully selected but were not the most valuable pieces. A necessary assumption is that art thieves would not carefully select such pieces for any reason other than for an individual collector. More generally, we could express this as "The manner of an art theft and the pieces stolen can indicate the destination of the stolen works." Even more generally, we could say, "The visible evidence of one's actions can indicate the purpose of those actions." Sometimes the correct answer will be more specific; sometimes it will be very general. You would be correct to anticipate either type of answer because the passage could serve as an example or illustration of both statements. Answer C) is correct and is similar to the

HELPFUL HINT

Review "Principles and Applications" in Chapter 1 to ensure that you thoroughly understand how general principles can apply to facts in order to produce conclusions.

first sentence. Answer A) is incorrect because it is a principle that would support the conclusion that an art theft was ordered by a known person or by a known group of people. The passage is not about who ordered the theft, and the passage does not argue that it was done for a known individual. Answer B) is incorrect because it is a mistaken reversal of what we want. This answer would work if the premise of the argument were that the theft was ordered by a single individual and if the conclusion were that the pattern of works taken and left alone must therefore defy rational analysis. Answer D) is incorrect because it would only apply to an argument whose premise was that an art theft was committed without a plan for disposing the works, and whose conclusion was that the works might therefore not include only the most valuable pieces. Answer E) is incorrect because it would support a conclusion about the integrity of an art collection, and that is not present in our argument.

★ 8. **E) is correct.** This passage contains two principles: "If an action is morally good, then it benefits another and it was intended to benefit another," and "If an action harms another and either the harm was intended or probable harm was reasonably foreseeable, then it is morally bad." Use a diagram to solve this passage.

MG → B + PI (morally good → benefit + intention to benefit another)

H + HI → MB (harm + intention of harm → morally bad)

H + RF → MB (harm + reasonable forethought → morally bad)

E) tells us that Jonathan did not intend to harm his niece. Jonathan agreed to watch his niece while she played and then became engrossed in conversation. During his conversation, his niece ran into the street and was hit and harmed by a bicycle. This is an example of the second principle ("If an action harms another and either the harm was intended or probable harm was reasonably foreseeable, then it is morally bad"). Jonathan's neglect harmed his niece *and*, although he did not intend the harm, reasonable forethought by Jonathan would have shown that becoming engrossed in conversation was likely to cause the harm. Therefore, E) is correct.

The diagram (H + RF → MB) matches our third conditional statement exactly.

Diagramming and Discussing the Incorrect Answers

A) tells us that Pamela intended harm. Pamela did not cause harm. Therefore, Pamela's action was morally bad. This is an incorrect example of the second principle because no actual harm occurred.

Diagram: NH + HI → cannot conclude behavior was bad, as no harm was caused.

B) tells us that Jeffrey benefited Sara, so Jeffrey's action is morally good. However, the answer does not tell us that Jeffrey *intended* to benefit Sara, so the first principle does not apply to the scenario. Thus, B) is incorrect.

Diagram: B → cannot conclude behavior was good. Though benefit (B) is a necessary condition for moral goodness, it is not sufficient to result in goodness.

C) tells us that Teresa intended to benefit her neighbor and inadvertently harmed him. Therefore, morally good actions can have bad consequences. This is wrong for two reasons. First, we cannot conclude that Teresa's action was morally good to begin with (do we know that her clearing the neighbor's walkway benefited him?). Second, neither one of our principles supports a conclusion about when actions have bad consequences. This conclusion does not follow as an example of the passage, so C) is incorrect.

Diagram: PI + H → cannot conclude anything given the conditional statements here, as our passages' principles do not align with the conditional statements provided.

D) tells us that Marilees benefited the homeless man by giving him her sandwich. Marilees unintentionally caused the homeless man harm when he choked. Therefore, Marilees performed a morally bad action. This comes close to exemplifying the second principle, but falls short. Marilees's action itself did not necessarily harm the homeless man (his attempt to talk appears to have caused the harm). Additionally, Marilees did not intend to harm him, and not even reasonable forethought could have predicted that the homeless man would choke on the sandwich. Thus, the sufficient condition of the second principle is not met, and the second principle does not apply. Answer D) is therefore incorrect.

Diagram: H → cannot conclude anything given the statements here, as we do not know whether Marilees could have foreseen the choking or intended the choking to happen.

★ 9. **A) is correct.** First, read the question stem. This is a Strengthen question, so look for ways to make the argument's conclusion more likely: *Which one of the following, if true, most strengthens the argument?*

Next, read the passage. The author's conclusion is the last sentence: *It is obvious, then, that there should be a general reduction in the pace of bringing to the marketplace new drugs that are now being tested.*

Now, consider how to strengthen the argument. Why does poor understanding of a new antihistamine support a general slowdown in the introduction of new drugs?

Review the answers. What is your reaction as you read answer A)? Many students immediately cross off A), saying to themselves something like "That can't be true." Consider, however, that the question just told us to assume that the answers *are* true (the question says, "Which of the following, if true…"). Accordingly, A) is the correct answer because it does exactly what we need it to: it tells us that even though the new antihistamine is poorly understood, it is still much better understood than other new drugs. Therefore, most of the other new drugs are understood even more poorly.

As you work through Hypothetical questions, take care not to read answers as *contradicting* the passage. You will never have an answer to a Hypothetical question that contradicts the passage. Instead, as in this example, consider how an *apparently contradictory* answer choice works *with* the information in the passage to produce a strengthening inference.

Many students read answer A) as contradicting (and thus weakening) the statement in the passage that the new antihistamine is not well understood.

 HELPFUL HINT

Many students choose answers B) or D) when solving this question. Answer B) is incorrect because it only says that "some" of the new drugs have a poorly understood social impact. This does not help support a conclusion that there should be a general, or overall, reduction in the pace of bringing new drugs to market.

But answer A) does not actually say that the antihistamine is well understood. It just says that it is better understood than the other new drugs.

Answer D) is incorrect because there is no logical basis for inferring that chemical similarity is the same as social impact. If you chose D), perhaps you were relying on your own outside information to justify your answer choice, which is a mistake.

All Hypothetical questions work in this way; they require you to choose an answer, not based on what the passage has already said, but based on what *would hypothetically* make the passage better or worse, without regard to the factual truth of the answer choice. The diagram that accompanies this family shows an arrow pointing *from* the answers *to* the passage (see Table 3.4). This represents the idea that you are adding new information into the passage. These questions gauge your ability to use inductive reasoning to choose an answer that supports, undermines, or reconciles the passage.

★ 10. **D) is correct.** This choice validates the assumption that reducing the speed limit on the highway actually makes highway fatalities less likely. This is a cause-and-effect argument. The effect, as always, is in the premises: the rate of highway fatalities dropped following the 1974 speed limit reduction. The author's purported cause, as always, is in the conclusion: the speed limit reduction *caused* the decrease in highway fatalities. This argument commits the fallacy of false cause. Anything else might have caused the decline in fatalities after 1974: people stopped driving, cars became safer, people started taking driver's education, and so on. If some of these statements are true, then it might be true that reducing the speed limit *increased* highway fatalities in a way that was hidden by the decrease caused by other factors. The point is that without more information, we cannot conclude that the speed limit reduction caused the decrease in fatalities. A) is incorrect because it brings in an alternate possible cause for the effect (people stopped driving, thus there were fewer highway fatalities) and is therefore a weakener. B) is incorrect because it is irrelevant: the fact that there was no further decline in fatalities in 1986 does not prove or disprove the cause of the decline during the previous eleven years. C) is incorrect for the same reason as choice A). It weakens the argument by presenting an alternate possible cause for the effect. E) is incorrect because it weakens the argument by invalidating the assumption that reducing the speed limit on the highway makes highway fatalities less likely. It does this by stating that uniformity in the speed of traffic, rather than a reduction in the speed limit, is more likely to decrease accidents.

★ 11. **C) is correct.** This choice is neither a strengthener nor a weakener. It discusses the effective pollination of ornamental trees, which are completely irrelevant to the conclusion. Keep in mind that this is an EXCEPT question. Instead of looking for an answer that strengthens the passage, look for four answers that weaken the passage. Eliminate those four answers to find the remaining—correct—one. The conclusion is that domestic honey production will not decline if we replace local American honeybees with Africanized honeybees. Unfortunately, the only premise we have to support this is that the Africanized honeybees were better honey producers than local Brazilian honeybees in Brazil. This is a terribly weak argument. To find weakeners, we first state the counterargument by negating the conclusion: domestic honey production might decline when the Africanized honeybees are introduced. The answer that strengthens this counterargument is our weakener. A) is a weakener because it indicates that the Africanized honeybees, while superior to the Brazilian bees, might not be superior to the American bees. B) is also a weakener. It indicates that commercial honey production will become more expensive (thus leading to a decline in production) with the Africanized bees. D) is a weakener because it indicates that fewer beekeepers will produce honey with the Africanized bees, resulting in a decline in production. D) is a weakener, because it indicates that the Africanized honeybees will not produce as well in America as in Brazil.

★ 12. **C) is correct.** This answer choice indicates that the company is only going to purchase cars that are already not running, with the net result being zero reduction in pollution. Answer A) is consistent with the passage and, therefore, incorrect. It even indicates that the author's proposal would be less burdensome than it first appears: by removing a mere 1 percent of the area's cars, it could potentially remove 30 percent of the air pollution. If you chose this answer as correct, you were likely thinking that it somehow negated the premise that "automobiles that predate 1980 account for 30 percent" of the pollution. However, the answer is consistent with this premise. Answer B) discusses costs, which the argument is not concerned about, and so is incorrect. Answer D) is incorrect because it is consistent with the argument. Answer E) is incorrect because it discusses citizen group complaints, which is irrelevant.

★ 13. **D) is correct.** Essentially, D) says, "Risky projects are undertaken only if there is a single decision-maker." This is correct because it is a logical equivalent (contrapositive) of the anticipated answer. Here, we have conditional statements. The premise is "If it is a bureaucracy, then there is no single decision-maker." The conclusion is "Therefore, if it is a bureaucracy, then there are no risky projects." We want an answer that fully justifies the conclusion, so ideally we would like a form of "If there is no single decision-maker, then there can be no risky projects." This would use the pure hypothetical argument form to produce this syllogism:

Stated Premise: "If it is a bureaucracy, then there is no single decision-maker."

Added Premise: "If there is no single decision-maker, then there can be no risky projects."

Conclusion: "Therefore, if it is a bureaucracy, then there are no risky projects."

This is a deductively valid argument that cannot be further strengthened or weakened. Based on the stated premise and our added premise, the conclusion follows inescapably and is perfectly justified.

A) is incorrect because it contradicts the conclusion of the argument. B) is incorrect because it allows for the possibility that risky projects might still be undertaken, even in the absence of decisive individuals. C) is incorrect because it is a mistaken negation of the desired answer. This says, "If there is an individual decision-maker, then that person will take risks." We want the opposite—if there is no individual decision-maker, then there will be no risks taken. The two sentences are not the same. E) is incorrect because people acting in groups being more averse to risk than those acting alone is irrelevant. It does not prove that bureaucracies lack risky projects.

★ 14. **B) is correct.** This is an EXCEPT question, so eliminate the four answers that resolve the apparent paradox. First, identify the paradox: all age groups considered R Bar Beans the best in the survey, but Texas T and Aunt Sally's Beans sell more cans than R Bar. B) does *not* resolve the paradox. It would not matter if some age groups liked R Bar Beans more than other beans by an even greater margin than other age groups did. Texas T and Aunt Sally's could still sell more cans of beans than R Bar.

The other answer choices could all resolve the paradox. As stated in answer A), perhaps R Bar Beans are prohibitively expensive, or as stated in answer C), perhaps they have a limited availability, whereas Texas T and Aunt Sally's are available everywhere. Maybe R Bar Beans are only available in specialty stores, and the brand refuses to share a shelf with other bean brands, reducing R Bar's availability—answer D). Or maybe the sales figures cover a long period of time during which lots of Texas T and Aunt Sally's Beans were sold, but not as many R Bar Beans were sold because R Bar Beans are new—answer E). These four answers all explain why R Bar Beans do not sell as well as the other beans, despite their greater popularity. They can all be ruled out as a result.

HELPFUL HINT

Many students struggle with becoming personally involved in the content of the argument or relating the content to what they know about the subject in real life. Reading the argument without the subject matter detail can break this habit and help in evaluating arguments dispassionately.

★ 15. **E) is correct.** First, paraphrase the passage as you read, omitting the subject matter detail. Simply describe what the author is doing: she presents a general historical statement about a country. She uses first person to describe a study she conducted about a country's habits. The author offers a present phenomenon as the consequence of the past habits she studied. The author concludes with a "moral of the story," invoking an analogy to prescribe a more desirable course of action or guiding principle for countries. Since this is an EXCEPT question, identify four argumentative strategies that the author uses. Answer A) is present: the dog eating its own tail is an analogue to a country living without trade. Answer B) is present: the second sentence is a historical fact. Answer C) is present: the foreign debt is the effect, and isolation from foreign trade is the cause. Answer D) is present: the foreign debt is a current economic situation. That leaves E), the correct choice. The author is *not* questioning the ethical basis of an economic situation.

★ 16. **C) is correct.** Here, the operative and first clause is "Homelessness is a serious social problem." The conclusion of the argument follows: government spending on low-income housing is not the cure for homelessness. The intermediate conclusion is the last sentence: homelessness is not caused by a lack of available housing. The premise is the middle sentence: there is no lack of available housing units. To reframe:

Premise: There is no lack of available housing units.

Intermediate Conclusion: So homelessness is not caused by a lack of available housing.

Main Conclusion: Therefore, government spending for low-income housing is not the cure for homelessness.

What is the function of the first clause? Essentially, it is background information—the politician's attempt to agree with one of his opponent's premises (homelessness is serious) while refuting an opposing conclusion that the government should spend money on housing. C) is therefore the correct answer because the clause in question is compatible with both the politician's argument and the argument of an opponent who would deny the politician's argument. A) and D) are incorrect because the politician does not deny that homelessness is serious. B) is incorrect because the argument does not resolve the problem. E) is incorrect because the clause is not a necessary assumption; it could be false without damaging the argument.

★ 17.   **B) is correct.** The fallacy here is false cause. The effect is that the mixture did not fizz. The author's alleged cause is that the bottle labeled "vinegar" was not actually vinegar. However, it is equally plausible that the box labeled baking soda was not actually baking soda. If the author had first stated, "And we know that the box actually contained baking soda," then the conclusion of a mislabeled bottle would be justified. However, the author failed to exclude a mislabeled box as an alternative explanation for the effect, creating a flawed argument. A) is incorrect because the author does not actually ignore the possibility that the bottle contained another acid—only that the bottle is mislabeled. However, it would not make sense for the author to address the possibility of the bottle containing another acid, because the passage stated that *any* acid would fizz if mixed with baking soda. Therefore, it would not be a fallacy for the author to ignore other acids because even another acid would have fizzed when mixed with baking soda. C) is incorrect because there is no reason to assume that *fizz* is an imprecise term; it is not used in two different ways in the argument. D) is incorrect because ignoring scientific principles about controlled experiments is not a fallacy. The argument is discussing the fizzing that should result from mixing acids and baking soda, not testing scientific principles. E) is incorrect because the author is not arguing that anyone intended to deceive anyone.

★ 18.   **E) is correct.** George is committing the fallacy of hasty generalization. Because of the unusually warm weather in his local area, he concludes the present occurrence of *global* warming. We need to know whether unseasonably warm weather is happening all around the globe—not only in George's area. If this were true, then George's conclusion would be strong. If this were false, then the conclusion would be weak. A) is incorrect because knowing carbon dioxide as the only cause of global warming does not help evaluate the present occurrence of global warming. B) is incorrect because knowing when the leaves usually change color does not matter. Regardless of when it usually happens, they were three weeks late. C) is incorrect because the cause of carbon dioxide emissions is irrelevant to the question of whether global warming is currently happening. D) is incorrect because even if air pollution is causing trees to lose their leaves, that does not counteract the unusually mild winter or the change in leaf color.

★ 19.   **A) is correct.** Here, we have conditional statements. The argument says, "If guilty, then Max would not ask. Max asked. Therefore, Max is not guilty."

HELPFUL HINT

Remember, you do not need to diagram all the answer choices. When you see conditional statements, try to diagram the passage to see the pattern of reasoning more clearly. Then, as you read through the answer choices, compare the answer choices to your shorthand diagram, matching components of the answer choices to the statements written in shorthand.

This is a perfectly valid argument in the contrapositive form. Many students respond to this question by saying, "That's not valid. Max could still be guilty even if he asked the police." But from a purely logical standpoint, the first premise expressly states that if Max were guilty, he would not ask the police to investigate. This conclusively excludes the possibility that Max could be guilty and still ask the police. It is perfectly reasonable for you to think that this premise would be false in the real world, but you must accept all premises on the LSAT as true.

In shorthand, the argument here is: G → ~A

A

∴ ~G

A) is the correct answer and can be diagrammed as follows:

N → ~S (N = next room; S = I am able to see her)

S

∴ ~N

This is an exact match of the valid pattern of reasoning in the passage.

★ **20. D) is correct.** Here, the question tells us that we are looking for two flaws. The first flaw is mistaken reversal:

I → N (I = intelligent; N = nearsighted) very N

∴ very I

The second flaw is confusing *correlation* with *condition*. To illustrate the second flaw, let's pretend that the first fallacy were fixed: change the first premise to all nearsighted people are intelligent. The problem is that not all those who are very nearsighted are necessarily very intelligent (the argument uses genius here as a synonym for very intelligent). The author is confusing a conditional statement for a correlation, and that is poor reasoning.

The correct answer is D):

T → H (T = tall; H = happy) very H

∴ very T

Remember, the order of the sentences does not matter. The conclusion was the last sentence in the passage, and it is the second clause in the answer, but you should untangle the premises and conclusions of the arguments so that you are reading them in the same order. This makes comparing the arguments easier.

Answer A) could be valid if it started with "I must not be intelligent" since that follows the Contrapositive form. Answer B) commits the mistaken reversal, but it does not confuse correlation and condition. Answer C) confuses correlation and condition, but it does not commit mistaken reversal. Answer E) is a valid argument.

★ **21. C) is correct.** As you read the passage, develop a general principle that the passage reflects. An appropriate principle would be something like "It is justifiable to ignore general expert advice where it might not apply to the decision-maker's specific situation." Then look for an answer that would be an example of that principle. A climber might not follow general expert advice about mountains when those experts are unfamiliar with the specific mountain in question. At the same time, a parent might ignore general expert advice about childrearing from experts unfamiliar with their children. A) is incorrect because it does not argue for taking or dismissing another's advice. B) does address not taking experts' advice, yet it is incorrect because its reasoning concerns whether the experts are interested in the same factors as the consumer—not whether the experts' advice is too general. D) is incorrect because it does not argue for taking or dismissing another's advice. E) is incorrect because it argues for heeding one's conscience over the voice of society. This is not in line with a principle about when it is justifiable to disregard *expert* advice.

The LSAT has one Analytical Reasoning section. These questions are also known as Logic Games. This chapter will discuss the different types of Logic Games and strategies for answering these questions correctly.

There are a few different types of logic games, but they all have the same structure. Let's start by identifying the components of a Logic Game in Table 4.1:

TABLE 4.1. Components of a Logic Game

COMPONENT	EXAMPLE
Source: For official LSAT questions, we have listed the PrepTest number from which the game is taken for your reference. Each game contains five to seven questions.	★ LSAT exam questions (PrepTest 16, questions 1 - 6)
Scenario: This paragraph tells you what you are doing in this game. Read closely and carefully. Are you putting variables in order? Dividing them into groups? This will determine the best diagram to use in drawing out the scenario and the rules.	Eight new students—R, S, T, V, W, X, Y, and Z—are being divided among exactly three classes: class 1, class 2, and class 3. Classes 1 and 2 will gain three new students each; class 3 will gain two new students. The following restrictions apply:
Rules: Although you are given some restrictions in the scenario (and these are important), there are always two to seven additional rules that apply to every question in the game. Understand exactly what each rule prohibits. Here, for example, the last rule prohibits a situation in which T is in class 1 without Z.	• R must be added to class 1. • S must be added to class 3. • Neither S nor W can be added to the same class as Y. • V cannot be added to the same class as Z. • If T is added to class 1, Z must also be added to class 1.
Questions: Each game has five to seven questions. Some provide additional information that pertains to that question only.	1. Which one of the following is an acceptable assignment of students to the three classes?

continued on next page

TABLE 4.1. Components of a Logic Game (continued)			
COMPONENT	**EXAMPLE**		
	1	2	3
Answer Choices: Each question will have five answer choices. Only one is correct. You will never have two good answers to choose from. Four will be wrong for an identifiable reason.	A) R, T, Y	V, W, X	S, Z
	B) R, T, Z	S, V, Y	W, X
	C) R, W, X	V, Y, Z	S, T
	D) R, X, Z	T, V, Y	S, W
	E) R, X, Z	V, W, Y	S, T

Methodology

For each game, apply the following method:

1. Read the scenario and skim the rules. Determine the best diagram (ordering, stacked, division, matching, in-and-out, or something unique).

2. Write down the variables.

3. Draw the shell of your diagram.

4. Write down each rule visually in a way that will help you apply it during the game.

5. When two rules affect a common variable, group, or location, you should stop and think carefully about whether you can infer any additional rules ("make deductions").

6. Identify any unrestricted variables ("floaters") that are not affected by the rules.

7. Answer the questions, returning to your handwritten rules as often as possible.

 DID YOU KNOW?

The biggest downfall of most LSAT test takers is working through every answer choice instead of actively solving the problems. The way to improve on the LSAT is to learn how the test works by solving each question.

Time Management

There are four games in the thirty-five-minute section, for a total of twenty-two to twenty-four questions.

On average, you should allot three minutes for diagramming each game's scenario and set of rules. Write down your variables, and write down how many variables you have. Diagram your rules in a useful way. Pretend that at the end of three minutes, the printed rules will disappear from the page and all you will have left is what you have written down. Spend this time understanding exactly what each rule prohibits.

Then, spend one minute or less on each of the questions. This will allow you to complete the twenty-three questions in the four games within the thirty-five minutes given.

Many questions ask, "If [new information] is true, then what else must be true?" On these questions, you must take the new information, write it down, work through your rules, and attempt to answer the question without even looking at your answer choices. The clue in the question is that the new information, if true, will lead you all the way to the answer. Follow that clue and solve the question as though it were fill-in-the-blank instead of multiple choice.

Space Management

You are not allowed any scratch paper on the LSAT, so it is important to be neat and organized as you draw your diagrams. In the examples that follow, notice (especially on Ordering and Division Games) that you should have your rules entirely separate from your workspace. Once you have gone to the trouble of mapping out your rules, do not ruin your diagram by working out a question in that same space. Instead, work out the questions next to or below the space where your rules are.

Unrestricted Variables

In many games, one or more variables have no rules that directly affect them. On questions asking, "What *could* be true?" these variables frequently appear in the correct answers, because they *could* go just about anywhere. On the other hand, where a question asks "What *must* be true?" these variables are less often the answer.

Old Games Versus New Games: How Has the LSAT Changed?

In June 1991, the LSAT was released in substantially the same form as it exists today, with a few changes:

1. Some older games include a predesigned diagram. For example: PrepTest 4/Game 4 and PrepTest 8/Game 2 include diagrams that look like connect the dots.

2. Older tests included a Process-type of game (not seen since the September 1995 LSAT), including scenarios where, for example, you arrange words in a sequence by adding, removing, or altering a letter in each word.

3. Recent games tend to be more straightforward than some of the older tests. However, some of the recent tests (such as PrepTest 62) have very difficult Logic Games.

The games you see on test day will likely be similar to the Logic Games that have been released in recent years. However, it is advisable to work through both old and new games to expose yourself to the full breadth of scenarios that have appeared in official modern (post-1991) LSATs.

Logic Games: Question Types

These are the primary question types that appear on any given game, regardless of game type:

1. general questions
2. "if" questions (hypothetical questions)
3. determination questions
4. change/substitute/add-a-rule questions

General Questions (Questions Asking About Your Original Scenario/Rules)

"WHAT MUST BE TRUE?"

The answer is something that must be true all the time. If you can show that an answer choice could be false, then it is not the answer. If the answer choice cannot be false, then it is the answer.

Strategy: Look at the rules first, and then take a quick glance through the five answer choices. The correct answer should be either a combination of two rules or a quick inference that you can make based on the rules.

"WHAT MUST BE FALSE?"

You are looking for a lie. If an answer choice could ever be true, then it is not the answer.

Strategy: Again, think about the rules. The correct answer must violate a rule, so think about the ways in which this can happen. Then take a quick glance through the five answers and start with the choices that stand out as potentially violating one of your rules.

"WHAT COULD BE TRUE?"

The answer is something that is possible under some circumstance, somehow. This tells you that the four wrong answers all must be false all the time. Often, the first question asks, "Which of the following could be an accurate scenario?" On these, instead of starting with answer A) and working through each option, take your rules one at a time, and eliminate the answer choices that violate each rule.

Strategy: When a "What Could Be True" question is the first question of the game, use each rule to eliminate an answer choice. On other "could be true" questions, just run through the five answers. Do it quickly, but thoroughly.

"WHAT COULD BE FALSE?"

The answer is something that does not have to be true. The four wrong answers *must be true*.

Strategy: Find four answers that must be true, eliminate them, and choose what is left.

Consider the equivalent questions in Table 4.2.

TABLE 4.2. Equivalent Questions

EXCEPT QUESTION	STANDARD QUESTION
Each of the following could be false EXCEPT =	Which of the following must be true?
Each of the following could be true EXCEPT =	Which of the following must be false?

EXCEPT QUESTION	STANDARD QUESTION
Each of the following must be false EXCEPT =	Which of the following could be true?
Each of the following must be true EXCEPT =	Which of the following could be false?

Hypothetical ("If") Questions

"If [new information] Is True, Then What Must Be True?"

For these questions, follow these steps:

1. Plug in the new information.

2. Look at rules that relate directly to the new information that you are given. For example, if they tell you "P goes in 3," you would look at all rules about P and all rules about space 3.

3. Then look at all of your remaining rules. Think about which other rules still need to "fit" somewhere in your diagram, especially blocks of consecutive or paired variables.

4. If they tell you that "P cannot go on Monday," you should think, "Who can go on Monday?"

5. If you can figure out where four out of five variables go, you should think about the fifth variable. Finish every one of your thought processes using the rules and your natural problem-solving skills.

6. Only then should you look at the answers. They are giving you the new information in the question to lead you to an answer choice. You should be able to take the new information and follow the rules to at least one more bit of information. Do this before you look at the answers, and you should have the answer before you see it.

7. One answer has to be true; there is no way out. (See "What Must Be True?" earlier in this section.)

"If [new information] Is True, Then What Could Be True?"

Try to treat these questions like the preceding. However, sometimes you still may not be able to figure out the exact answer. Plug in the new information, look at the relevant rules, and work through the remaining rules. If you cannot immediately spot the answer, then work through the answer choices. Eliminate the four answers that must be false.

Determination Questions

"Which of the Following, If True, Would Fully Determine Where the Other Variables Go?"

Strategy: Plug in the answers to see which one causes a domino effect such that every other variable goes into a spot with 100 percent certainty. If you have unrestricted variables, start with one of them.

Change/Substitute/Add-a-Rule Questions

"ASSUME THE RULE THAT [OLD RULE] IS REPLACED WITH THE CONDITION THAT [NEW RULE]. IF ALL OF THE OTHER CONDITIONS REMAIN THE SAME, THEN WHICH OF THE FOLLOWING MUST BE TRUE?"

Strategy: If you are changing a rule, erase the old rule from your diagram (along with any inferences you made from it) and add in the new rule. If you are asked to substitute an equally effective rule, understand that you are being asked to reword the rule. Look for an answer that rephrases the rule in different terms. If you are asked to add a rule, just tack it on and look for any additional deductions you can make.

HELPFUL HINT

The next pages will walk through examples of all the types of Logic Games. You may wish to try the questions yourself before reading through. Time yourself at eight minutes and forty-five seconds per game, and attempt to complete the questions before moving on. You may use one sheet of plain white paper for each game (one side only). Draw the rules in a way that seems natural to you.

Do not try to keep everything in your head. This is a test of thoroughness. Your ability to analyze the problem and spot inferences is more important than rushing through the game. Usually, in an attempt to beat the clock, students sacrifice accuracy. First build accuracy; then build speed.

Game Types

Here we will look at five simple diagrams that can be used to sketch out almost any LSAT Logic Game. Most Logic Games fall into one of these five groups:

Ordering Games: These games involve variables that are being placed in a sequence. An example might be six people standing in line or seven cars finishing in a race (ranked first to last).

Stacked Games: These games can involve ordering multiples sets of variables at the same time. An example might be determining the rankings of seven cars in a race as well as the cars' colors. These games may also involve multidimensional ordering of a single set of variables. An example might be scheduling eight classes on Monday through Thursday mornings and afternoons. Finally, these games may involve several sets of variables without an element of ordering at all. "Stacked" is more of a type of *organizational system* than an actual type of game. These are not stacking games, but rather stacked diagrams.

Division Games: These games involve separating a large group of variables into smaller subgroups. An example might be grouping six children by whether they play soccer, tennis, or volleyball.

Matching Games: These games involve identifying the characteristics that apply to each variable in a group. An example might be identifying which of the six children speak English, French, and/or Spanish. The difference between this and a Division Game is that here, the children could potentially speak more than one language. Thus, there is no actual division into groups. If each child could only speak one language, then this would be a Division Game.

In-and-Out Games: These games involve separating a large group of variables into a subgroup that is "in" and a subgroup that is "out." The rules are generally conditional statements.

There are also "other" games. Almost every Logic Game released since 1991 fits into one of the preceding five categories. The handful of games that do not generally come from the 1990s. While these games test the same general skills, you may find it useful to complete them to expose yourself to the full breadth of scenarios that have appeared on official LSAT tests. See "Game Type 6: Other Games" for a discussion of the various other games that have appeared.

Game Type One: Ordering Games

In Ordering Games, you are arranging some sequence of variables from first to last, old to new, top to bottom, and so on. Words like *before* and *after* occur frequently in the rules.

Let's look at a standard Ordering Game.

★ LSAT EXAM QUESTIONS

PrepTest 1: Questions 14 – 18

The eight partners of a law firm are Gregg, Hodges, Ivan, James, King, MacNeil, Nader, and Owens. In each of the years 1961 through 1968, exactly one of the partners joined the firm.

- Nader joined the firm before Owens.
- James joined the firm before MacNeil.
- Gregg joined the firm before Ivan.
- Hodges joined the firm before Nader
- King joined the firm before James.
- Nader and James joined the firm before Gregg.

14. Which one of the following CANNOT be true?
    A) Hodges joined the law firm in 1961.
    B) Hodges joined the law firm in 1963.
    C) Gregg joined the law firm in 1964.
    D) MacNeil joined the law firm in 1964.
    E) Owens joined the law firm in 1964.

15. If James joined the firm in 1962, which one of the following CANNOT be true?
    A) Hodges joined the firm in 1963.
    B) MacNeil joined the firm in 1963.
    C) Hodges joined the firm in 1964.
    D) Nader joined the firm in 1964.
    E) Owens joined the firm in 1964.

16. Of the following, which one is the latest year in which James could have joined the firm?
    A) 1962
    B) 1963
    C) 1964
    D) 1965
    E) 1966

17. If Owens joined the firm in 1965 and MacNeil joined in 1967, one can determine the years in which exactly how many of the other partners joined the firm?
    A) one
    B) two

C) three

D) four

E) five

18. Assume that Owens joined the law firm before MacNeil. Of the following, which one is the earliest year in which MacNeil could have joined it?

    A) 1963

    B) 1964

    C) 1965

    D) 1966

    E) 1967

Note the question types. Question 14 is a **general** question ("What must be false?"). Question 15 is a **hypothetical** question ("If J is in 1962, then what must be false?"). Question 16 is another general question ("What is the latest that J could join?"). Question 17 is another hypothetical question ("If O is in 1965 and M is in 1967, *then* what do you know?"). Finally, question 18 is an **add-a-rule** question ("Add [O comes before M]. Now what is the earliest M could join?").

Also, notice that the variables each begin with a different letter. This is always the case.

Diagramming Ordering Games

Exhibit 1 is a sample diagram for the standard Ordering Game presented above. Note that the variables—the letters G, H, I, J, K, M, N, and O—all correspond to the names of the partners. Exhibit 2 shows the steps for connecting the rules.

Exhibit 1.
Variables: G H I J K M N O

Rules ⟶
$$H-N \begin{smallmatrix} O \\ G-I \\ M \end{smallmatrix}$$
$$K-J$$

Workspace ⟶
1	2	3	4	5	6	7	8

Exhibit 2.

H – N   H – N   H – N ⟍ G
        K – J   K – J

Do not write NJ – G.

H – N ⟨ O/G   H – N ⟨ O/G/M   H – N ⟨ O/G–I/M
K – J   K – J   K – J

1. H is before N.

2. K is before J.

3. N and J are before G.

4. N is before O.

5. J is before M.

6. G is before I.

Combine your rules as you go. Follow the preceding steps as you read each rule. When you read the third rule, "N and J are before G," your inclination should be to connect this rule to the N and the J already written on your page.

Use a simple dash to denote "before and after." Do not use an arrow (this will become confusing with "if...then" statements) or a < (less than)/> (greater than) symbol (this will become confusing when you actually have a game with greater than/less than).

Make a clean workspace. Master rules should go above your diagram. Use the space below the numbers (1 through 8) to work through individual scenarios as needed.

Be efficient. Instead of writing "1961, 1962, ... 1968," just use 1 through 8. Stop at the end of the rules and ask yourself questions like these:

- Who could be first? *Answer: H or K*
- Who could be second? *Answer: H, K, N, or J*
- Who could be last? *Answer: O, I, or M*
- What is the latest that H could be? *Answer: 1964 (before N, O, G, and I)*
- What is the earliest that G could be? *Answer: 1965 (after H, K, N, and J)*

Students who score high on the LSAT tend to spend as much time analyzing the scenario and the rules as they do solving the questions. Ask yourself questions like these before moving on to the first question.

Also, if you could not answer any of these questions correctly, fix your diagram. If, for example, you did not think that H could be as late as 1964, make sure that your diagram does not incorrectly indicate that H must come before M. Based on the rules, H can come either before M or after M. There is no rule connecting H and M, so do not make one up.

Use questions you have already solved in a logic game to solve other questions within that same game. If there is a universal "must be true" rule that applies to the entire game, use that universal answer choice and treat it as a new rule. Likewise, if there is a question for which you realize that an option can "never be true," that should be added as a new rule as well. Hypothetical questions can be used throughout the game to help you see possibilities for other questions. (If you have already diagrammed that X can sit next to Y, then you can answer with confidence later in the game that it is possible for X to sit next to Y, or at least know that diagram is a possibility and use this knowledge as a timesaver.)

Watch out for these common pitfalls:

Do not write all of the rules and *then* attempt to go back and combine them. This wastes time and risks errors on your part. Take the rules one at a time, and look for deductions as you work.

Do not wrongly view the rules in "columns" that do not exist. Here, for example, nothing says that I has to come after O and M. The only rule about I is that it must come after G. If you initially thought that I had to be last, you made up a rule that does not exist. Be careful not to do this.

Ordering Games: Analyzing the Answers

Diagram the game before reading through all the questions.

It is usually best to work through the questions in order, skipping and returning to any that you find difficult at first. However, if you find the hypothetical questions easier to solve, then you may consider doing those first before completing the remaining questions, or vice versa.

Game Type Two: Stacked Games

Stacked games encompass different sets of elements. "Stacked" refers to the way the diagram is drawn; each element is stacked in rows as in the following examples.

There are generally three kinds of scenarios in which a stacked diagram would be an appropriate organizational tool for a game:

1. You are ordering more than one set of variables.

    Example

    Exactly five cars—A, B, C, D, and E—compete in Martown's annual race. Exactly five drivers—Tang, Umiko, Victor, Wendy, and Xavier—drive the five cars. As the cars finish the race, they are ranked from first to last. There are no ties.

    Summarize the situation in one sentence to guide the setup:

    "In each of five places, there is a car and a driver."

    Exhibit 3.

	1	2	3	4	5
cars ABCDE					
drivers TUVWX					

    Example

    Exactly three cities are on the Harlan Executive Committee's tour: Albertville, Barcelona, and Calais. A total of six executives—J, K, L, N, P, and Q—will visit the cities on the tour, with exactly two executives visiting each city. Only one city is visited on each of Monday, Tuesday, and Wednesday.

    Summarize the situation in one sentence to guide the setup:

    "On each of three days, there is one city and there are two executives."

    Exhibit 4.

	M	T	W
cities ABC			
executives JKLNPQ			

2. You are ordering one set of variables in a multidimensional system.

Example

Marissa must take six courses: biology, chemistry, economics, French, history, and linguistics. She takes one course in the morning and one course in the afternoon on each of Tuesday, Wednesday, and Thursday. She does not take any courses on any other days of the week.

Summarize the situation in one sentence to guide the setup:

"On each of three days, there is a course in the morning and a course in the afternoon."

Exhibit 5.

	T	W	Th
am			
pm			

$BCEFHL_6$

3. You have one set of variables and two sets of constant elements. There is no ordering involved, but otherwise you have a situation like in the practice example.

Let's look at a standard Stacked Game.

★ **LSAT EXAM QUESTIONS**

PrepTest 1, Questions 19 – 24

The railway company has exactly three lines: line 1, line 2, and line 3. The company prints three sets of tickets for January and three sets of tickets for February: one set for each of its lines for each of the two months. The company's tickets are printed in a manner consistent with the following conditions:

- Each of the six sets of tickets is exactly one of the following colors: green, purple, red, or yellow.
- For each line, January tickets are a different color than February tickets.
- For each month, tickets for different lines are in different colors.
- Exactly one set of January tickets is red.
- For line 3, either January tickets or February tickets (but not both) are green.
- January tickets for line 2 are purple.
- No February tickets are purple.

19. If the line 3 tickets for January are red, then which one of the following statements must be true?

A) Line 1 tickets for January are green.

B) Line 1 tickets for January are yellow.

C) Line 1 tickets for February are red.

D) Line 2 tickets for February are yellow.

E) Line 3 tickets for February are green.

20. If one set of the line 2 tickets is green, then which of the following must be true?

   A) Line 1 tickets for January are red.

   B) Line 3 tickets for January are red.

   C) Line 1 tickets for February are red.

   D) Line 3 tickets for February are green.

   E) Line 3 tickets for February are yellow.

21. Which of the following could be true?

   A) No January ticket is green.

   B) No February ticket is green.

   C) Only line 2 tickets are red.

   D) One set of January tickets is green and one set of January tickets is yellow.

   E) The line 2 tickets for January are the same color as the line 1 tickets for February.

22. Which of the following could be true?

   A) Both line 1 tickets for January and line 2 tickets for February are green.

   B) Both line 1 tickets for January and line 2 tickets for February are yellow.

   C) Both line 1 tickets for January and line 3 tickets for February are yellow.

   D) Line 1 tickets for January are green, and line 3 tickets for February are red.

   E) Line 3 tickets for January are yellow, and line 1 tickets for February are red.

23. If the line 3 tickets for February are yellow, then each of the following must be true EXCEPT

   A) one set of January tickets is green.

   B) one set of line 1 tickets is red.

   C) one set of line 2 tickets is red.

   D) the tickets in two of the six sets are red.

   E) the tickets in two of the six sets are yellow.

24. Suppose that none of the ticket sets are purple. If all of the other conditions remain the same, then which one of the following statements could be true?

   A) None of the January tickets are green.

   B) None of the February tickets are green.

   C) None of the line 2 tickets are green.

   D) No line 1 or line 2 tickets are yellow.

   E) No line 2 or line 3 tickets are red.

Remember, you are dealing with three sets of elements: two months, three train lines, and four colors.

Diagramming Stacked Games

Here is the setup for this Stacked Game:

Note that there are only six sets of tickets; therefore, you should have six boxes in which you will fill in colors. Here, we know that there are three lines. In each line, there is one set of tickets for January and one set of tickets for February.

The unknown is the color of each set of tickets. Even though we know we have four colors, we do not know how many red, green, purple, or yellow sets of tickets there are.

Exhibit 6.

Master Diagram:

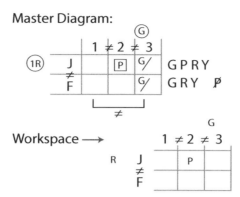

Workspace →

First, write "1 R in January" visually next to January. Then, write "1 G in line 3" above line 3, or as G in January, line 3, and February, line 3. There is no purple in February; this tells you that you will have one each of G, R, and Y.

Your goal is to construct an effective diagram with the fewest spaces possible; here, we need six spaces because there are six sets of tickets. A diagram with more (like eighteen or twenty-four) spaces in it would be inefficient and cumbersome.

Summarize the situation in one sentence to guide the setup:

> "In each of [#] [spaces], there is [an element] and [another element];
> fill in the [variables]."

For this example, the sentence could read:

> "In each of three lines, there is a set of tickets for January and a set for
> February. Fill in the colors."

Review the other stacked diagram examples above and consider the sentence that accompanies each diagram. The "fill in the variables" clause is only present when you have a single set of variables that you are organizing within a two-dimensional system.

💡 **HELPFUL HINT**

Do not mess with your master diagram once you have put it together. Make a separate workspace for hypothetical questions; either make a new diagram for each question or use your eraser.

Game Type Three: Division Games

In Division Games, you are taking elements of a larger group and assigning them into subgroups. Each element goes into one subgroup only.

Let's look at a standard Division Game. (Recall this game from the start of the chapter.)

PrepTest 16, Questions 1 – 6

Eight new students—R, S, T, V, W, X, Y, and Z—are being divided among exactly three classes: class 1, class 2, and class 3. Classes 1 and 2 will gain three new students each; class 3 will gain two new students. The following restrictions apply:

- R must be added to class 1.
- S must be added to class 3.
- Neither S nor W can be added to the same class as Y.
- V cannot be added to the same class as Z.
- If T is added to class 1, Z must also be added to class 1.

1. Which one of the following is an acceptable assignment of students to the three classes?

	1	2	3
A)	R, T, Y	V, W, X	S, Z
B)	R, T, Z	S, V, Y	W, X
C)	R, W, X	V, Y, Z	S, T
D)	R, X, Z	T, V, Y	S, W
E)	R, X, Z	V, W, Y	S, T

2. Which one of the following is a complete and accurate list of classes to which V could be added?

A) class 1
B) class 3
C) class 1, class 3
D) class 2, class 3
E) class 1, class 2, class 3

3. If X is added to class 1, which one of the following is a student who must be added to class 2?

A) T
B) V
C) W
E) Y
E) Z

4. If X is added to class 3, each of the following is a pair of students who can be added to class 1 EXCEPT

A) Y and Z.
B) W and Z.
C) V and Y.
D) V and W.
E) T and Z.

5. If T is added to class 3, which one of the following is a student who must be added to class 2?

A) V

B) W

C) X

D) Y

E) Z

6. Which one of the following must be true?

A) If T and X are added to class 2, V is added to class 3.

B) If V and W are added to class 1, T is added to class 3.

C) If V and W are added to class 1, Z is added to class 3.

D) If V and X are added to class 1, W is added to class 3.

E) If Y and Z are added to class 2, X is added to class 2.

Diagramming Division Games

Here is a sample diagram for the standard Division Game presented above:

Analyzing Division Games

1. Use a single diagram for your rules and your workspace.

   As with Ordering Games, you can save space by using a single diagram to represent the rules and to provide workspace for solving hypothetical questions.

2. Separate the rules from your workspace.

   Create a master scenario to depict the rules like "R is in class 1 and S is in class 3." Draw in spaces to show that there are three spaces in class 1 and class 2 and two spaces in class 3.

3. Diagram your rules visually.

   Notice how the last rule is drawn visually in the diagram. This is preferable to drawing something like "T1 → Z1" in the margin where you are likely to forget it.

4. Consider determining factors.

   Again, students who score well on the LSAT tend to spend as much time analyzing the scenario and the rules as they do solving the questions. Part of this analysis is understanding what additional information would produce meaningful deductions and what additional information would not be as meaningful.

For example, notice how there is only one open space in class 3, while there are two open spaces in class 1 and three open spaces in class 2. Would it be more useful to know that another variable (perhaps X) is in class 2 or class 3?

Exhibit 7.

Rules: S̶4̶
         W̶4̶
         V̶2̶

Workspace:

1	2	3
(T → 2)		
R _ _	_ _ _	S _ 4̶

 HELPFUL HINT

Do not confuse Division Games with Matching Games. The hallmark of a Division Game is that all of the elements are being assigned to *exactly* one subgroup. In Matching Games (below), the elements may go to more than one subgroup (usually, the prompt will tell you that each of the elements belongs to at least one category). It is inefficient to draw a Division Game like a Matching Game. The Logic Games Setup Exercise should help you with this.

The answer is class 3 because adding X to class 3 would require all of the remaining variables to fit into class 1 and class 2. Why does this matter? W and Y would have to be kept separate, as would V and Z. These variables would take up two spaces in each of class 1 and class 2. The remaining variable, T, would then be *forced* into class 2. If you had put X in class 2, nothing would have happened, but by putting X in class 3, you are able to make a meaningful deduction.

As you practice, try to develop an intuitive grasp of the kinds of factors that will determine additional information in a game.

Game Type Four: Matching Games

In Matching Games, you are determining which of several attributes apply to each of the variables. The key distinction of Matching Games is that each variable might possess more than one attribute, *and* each attribute might be possessed by more than one variable.

Look for language like, "Each of exactly six individuals plays *at least one* of three instruments." This phrasing indicates a Matching Game. If the scenario were "Each of six individuals plays *exactly one* of three instruments," then you would have a Division Game.

★ LSAT EXAM QUESTIONS

PrepTest 4, Questions 7 – 11

Each of five illnesses—J, K, L, M, and N—is characterized by at least one of the following symptoms: fever, headache, and sneezing. None of the illnesses has any symptom that is not one of these three.

- Illness J is characterized by headache and sneezing.
- Illnesses J and K have no symptoms in common.
- Illnesses J and L have at least one symptom in common.
- Illness L has a greater number of symptoms than illness K.
- Illnesses L and N have no symptoms in common.
- Illness M has more symptoms that illness J.

7. Which one of the following statements must be false?

   A) Illness J has exactly two symptoms.

   B) Illness K has exactly one symptom.

   C) Illness L has exactly two symptoms.

   D) Illness M has exactly three symptoms.

   E) Illness N has exactly two symptoms.

8. In which one of the following pairs could the first member of the pair be characterized by exactly the same number and types of symptoms as the second member of the pair?

   A) J and N

   B) K and L

C) K and N

   D) L and M

   E) M and N

9. If illness L is characterized by a combination of symptoms different from any of the other illnesses, then which one of the following statements must be true?

   A) Fever is a symptom of illness L.

   B) Sneezing is a symptom of illness L.

   C) Headache is a symptom of illness L.

   D) Illnesses K and N are characterized by exactly the same symptoms.

   E) Illnesses M and N are characterized by exactly the same symptoms.

10. Which pair of illnesses must have exactly one symptom in common?

    A) J and L

    B) J and M

    C) J and N

    D) K and L

    E) M and N

11. If Walter has exactly two of the three symptoms, then he cannot have all of the symptoms of

    A) both illness J and illness L.

    B) both illness J and illness N.

    C) both illness K and illness L.

    D) both illness K and illness N.

    E) both illness L and illness N.

Diagramming Matching Games

Here is a simple diagram for the standard Matching Game presented above:

Consider the scenario: Each of five illnesses has *at least one* of three symptoms. Using a division setup here would not be as effective because we are not simply dividing the five illnesses into three groups; rather, each illness might have multiple symptoms.

Exhibit 8.

1⁺/ea

	J	K	L	M	N
F	X	✓		✓	
L	✓	X	✓	✓	
L	✓	X	✓	✓	

J ≠ K   K<N   L ≠ N

Unlike in a Division Game, knowing that one of the illnesses here has fever as a symptom does *not* tell us whether that illness has any other symptoms as well. Accordingly, we use a diagram that allows us to depict three things:

   1. An illness *has* the symptom (a check mark).

   2. An illness *does not have* the symptom (an X).

   3. It is *unknown* whether the illness has the symptom (an empty box).

Next, connect the rules.

Exhibit 9.

1+/ea

	J	K	L	M	N
F					
H					
S					

1+/ea

	J	K	L	M	N
F					
H	✓				
S	✓				

1+/ea

	② J	① K	L	M	N
F	X	✓			
H	✓	X			
S	✓	X			

J ≠ K

1+/ea

	② J	① K	L	M	N
F	X	✓			
H	✓	X	⁄		
S	✓	X	⁄		

J ≠ K

1+/ea

	② J	① K	②⁺ L	M	N
F	X	✓			
H	✓	X	⁄		
S	✓	X	⁄		

J ≠ K   K<L

1+/ea

	② J	① K	② L	M	① N
F	X	✓			
H	✓	X	⁄		
S	✓	X	⁄		

J ≠ K   L ≠ N   K<L

1+/ea

	② J	① K	② L	③ M	① N
F	X	✓		✓	
H	✓	X	⁄	✓	
S	✓	X	⁄	✓	

J ≠ K   K<L

HELPFUL HINT

In any Matching Game, it is worth knowing how many attributes each variable can have.

DID YOU KNOW?

Make your diagram big enough that you can erase. Matching diagrams can be time consuming to draw. If you find it easier to draw new diagrams for each "if" question, then do so. If not, make your diagram large enough to allow you to work through several hypothetical scenarios within it, erasing between each one.

1. Each illness has at least one symptom.

2. J has H (headache) and S (sneezing).

3. J and K have nothing in common. Infer that K does not have H or S. However, K must have at least one symptom, so K must have F (fever). Infer that J does not have F.

4. J and L have at least one symptom in common. Use a dot or some symbol to note that L must have either H or S (it could have both).

5. L has more than K. Infer that L has two or more symptoms.

6. L and N have nothing in common. Infer that N can only have one symptom (if it had two or more, then it would be impossible for L to have two or more). Infer from this that L must have exactly two symptoms.

7. M has more than J. Infer that M has all symptoms.

Process each rule. Analyze each one before moving on; then carefully consider what it is prohibiting.

Look for numerical constraints. Rules like "L and N have no symptoms in common" should make you consider (1) which symptoms they have and (2) how many symptoms they have. It is worth noting how many symptoms each variable can have.

Game Type Five: In-and-Out Games

In-and-Out Games are characterized by a series of conditional rules. Your primary goal in an In-and-Out Game is to determine which variables out of a group are in and which are out. For example, you might have seven candidates for a promotion, and only some of them will earn the promotion. Your goal is to determine which candidates are in the group that earns the promotion, and which candidates are in the group that does not. Or you might have eight schoolteachers, some of whom will be in the group going on a field trip while some will not.

In many ways, these games are a subset of Division Games because you are dividing a group of variables into two subgroups: those in and those out. We treat these In-and-Out Games as their own category, however, because the rules of In-and-Out games are overwhelmingly conditional in nature. That is, all or most of the rules are hypothetical statements starting with "if" or containing an "only if" or "unless." Review conditional statements and the fallacies of mistaken reversal and mistaken negation to ensure that you do not make any reasoning errors while you read the rules in these games.

To diagram a rule such as "If Alex goes to the football game, then so will Becky," we will use the simple notation "If A, then B" (A → B). If it helps, you can choose to read this as "If A is true, then B is true." Rather than writing out, "A is true," many people simply use the letter A.

Let's look at a standard In-and-Out Game.

★ **LSAT EXAM QUESTIONS**

In-and-Out Game, Questions 1 – 7

A hiking group has exactly seven members: Hannah, Isaac, John, Kevin, Linda, Mike, and Nancy. The group must decide which members will participate in the next hiking event, subject to the following conditions:

- If Kevin participates, then so does Isaac.
- If Mike does not participate, then Hannah must participate.
- Isaac cannot participate unless Linda also participates.
- Neither John nor Hannah participates in any hiking event in which Linda participates.

1. Which one of the following could be a complete and accurate list of the members who participate in the next hiking event?
   A) Hannah, John, Kevin, Nancy
   B) Hannah, Linda, Mike, Nancy
   C) Hannah, Isaac, John, Linda
   D) Isaac, Linda, Mike, Nancy
   E) Isaac, John, Kevin, Mike

2. If both Kevin and Nancy participate in the next hiking event, then exactly how many of the other members must also participate?

    A) zero

    B) one

    C) two

    D) three

    E) four

3. If exactly three members participate in the next hiking event, each of the following could be true EXCEPT

    A) John and Mike both participate.

    B) Hannah and Nancy both participate.

    C) Isaac and Nancy both participate.

    D) Isaac and Linda both participate.

    E) Mike and Nancy both participate.

4. What is the maximum number of members who could participate in the next hiking event if Mike does not?

    A) two

    B) three

    C) four

    D) five

    E) six

5. If both John and Nancy participate, then which of the following must be true?

    A) Linda also participates.

    B) Isaac also participates.

    C) Mike also participates.

    D) Kevin does not participate.

    E) Hannah does not participate.

6. If Linda does not participate, each of the following could be true EXCEPT:

    A) both John and Nancy participate.

    B) both John and Mike participate.

    C) exactly three members participate.

    D) exactly four members participate.

    E) both Kevin and Hannah participate.

7. Suppose that the condition that if Mike does not participate then Hannah must participate is removed and is replaced with the condition that only if Nancy participates can Kevin fail to participate. If all other conditions remain in effect, what is the maximum number of members other than Kevin who could participate in the next hiking event with Kevin?

    A) one

    B) two

C) three

D) four

E) five

The In-and-Out Games Method

A solid method is crucial to solving In-and-Out Games quickly. Apply the following method and try to develop a solid understanding of the rules of each game.

1. Write down all the variables, from top to bottom, on the left side of your workspace.

2. Write each rule one at a time, stopping after each rule to apply each of the following steps.

3. If you have just written a rule with a negative term, write the contrapositive form by flipping the variables and negating them. The negated form of A is ~A; the negated form of ~B is B. No matter the conditional statement, it will always be fully equivalent in meaning to its contrapositive form.

4. Look for connections where two rules have the same variable in common, and carry over inferences. For example, let's say you were given these two rules: "Alex will not go to the picnic unless Becky goes" and "Only if Charlie goes to the picnic will Becky go."

   We would write these two rules like this: "A → B" and "B → C."

   These rules have B in common. If you have A, you have B. Add "If A, then C" to your rules simply by adding C to the right of the arrow that extends from A. This is carrying over an inference.

   Instead of writing "A → C" as a separate rule, combine this inference with the rules about A that you already have. This way, when A is in, you can look at your rules for A and know that both B and C must also be in. Therefore:

   A → B C

   B → C

5. When you carry over a *negative* term, write its *contrapositive* form.

   Although the preceding five-step method is fairly mechanical, try to let your common sense prevail when it comes to things like understanding the rules of logic games. Many course guides will teach you formulas, which can actually hinder your success if you encounter a seemingly new situation and cannot figure out how to apply the formula.

Be sure to stay organized. Step 1 requires you to write *all* of your variables vertically before you get started. This way, by the time you have worked through the rules, you will have a clear grasp of which variables have many, few, or no consequences.

 DID YOU KNOW?

Students make the most errors when they rush through the rules instead of looking for meaningful inferences. This is especially true for In-and-Out Games.

 HELPFUL HINT

Only write the contrapositive form of a rule when it contains a negative term. Writing the contrapositive forms of conditional rules is a good habit; it will help you make inferences, which means it will help you see how multiple rules work together.

Applying the In-and-Out Games Method

When you work through specific questions, it can be useful to use a T-chart or other organizational tool to distinguish who is in from who is out.

Step 1: Write your variables: H I J K L M N

Step 2: Write your rules, one at a time.

> **First Rule (K → I):**
>
> H I J
>
> K → I
>
> L M N

Step 3 (First Rule): Write the contrapositive if there is a negative term (we have none here, so we move on).

Step 4 (First Rule): Make connections (we only have one rule so far, so we move on).

Step 5 (First Rule): We did not make any connections, so we move on.

> **Second Rule (~M → H): H I J**
>
> K → I L
>
> M   ~M → H
>
> N

Step 3 (Second Rule): Write the contrapositive if there is a negative term (there is not one here, so we move on).

> H   ~H → M
>
> I J
>
> K → I L
>
> M   ~M → H
>
> N

Step 4 (Second Rule): Make connections (no two rules share a common variable, so we move on).

Step 5 (Second Rule): We did not make any connections, so we move on.

> **Third Rule (I → L):**
>
> H   ~H → M
>
> I → L
>
> J
>
> K → I L
>
> M   ~M → H
>
> N

Step 3 (Third Rule): Write the contrapositive if there is a negative term (there is not one here, so we move on).

Step 4 (Third Rule): Make connections. "If K then I, and if I then L share I." Infer "If K then L":

```
H      ~H → M
I        → L J
K → I L
L
M      ~M → H
N
```

Step 5 (Third Rule): We did not carry over any negative terms, so we move on.

```
Fourth Rule (L → ~J ~H):
H      ~H → M
I        → L J
K → I L
L → ~J ~H
M      ~M → H
N
```

Step 3 (Fourth Rule): Write the contrapositives. Here, we have two ("J → ~L" and "H → ~L"):

```
H → ~L          ~H → M
I → L
J → ~L
K → I L
L → ~J ~H
M      ~M → H
N
```

Step 4 (Fourth Rule): Make connections. Notice that the rule we are dealing with ("If L then no J and no H") is triggered by the presence of L and that two other variables (I and K) require L. Therefore, "If I then no J and no H and If K then no J and no H." Carry over these inferences:

```
H → ~L          ~H → M
I → L ~J ~H
J → ~L
K → I L ~J ~H
L → ~J ~H
M      ~M → H
N
```

Additionally, everywhere that you have a "not H" you know that you must have an M (because we have a rule that says "If H is out, then M is in"):

```
H → ~L          ~H → M
I → L ~J ~H M
J → ~L
K → I L ~J ~H M
L → ~J ~H M
M        ~M → H
N
```

Step 5 (Fourth Rule): For the negative terms (~J and ~H) that we just carried over (to I and to K), write the contrapositive forms:

```
H → ~L ~I ~K   ~H → M I → L ~J ~H M
J → ~L ~I ~K
K → I L ~J ~H M L → ~J ~H M
M        ~M → H
N
```

At first, this may seem like a lot just to read through the rules of a logic game—especially one you are supposed to complete in less than nine minutes. However, once you can diagram the rules, write appropriate contrapositives, and make connections in three or four minutes, you will find that it is time well spent. With a solid method for interpreting and connecting the rules, most of the questions presented should not be difficult. However, work through the sample In-and-Out Game several times. That way, you will build up your familiarity and speed with the method.

Game Type Six: Other Games

Most logic games fit into one of the five game types already discussed: Ordering, Stacked, Division, Matching, and In-and-Out. Some games, however, do not. These others fall into one of four groups: Hybrid Games (combinations of two of the five primary game types), Diagram Games, Process Games, and Miscellaneous Games.

Hybrid Games

There are only a very few true Hybrid Games, which test your ability to perform two of the primary game functions in the same scenario. Many LSAT courses refer to difficult games as hybrid, especially when the games may involve conditional rules or many sets of variables. Many of these so-called Hybrid Games, however, can be set up easily as Stacked Games.

Diagram Games

Seven of the older (1992–1997) LSAT tests include games that provide a visual diagram in the scenario itself, as part of the rules. It is unlikely, though not impossible, that such games will appear on your LSAT.

Process Games

Five of the older (1992–1995) LSAT tests include games that require you to apply a "process," such as changing letters in a sequence of words or mixing chemicals to change their colors. It is unlikely, though not impossible, that such games will appear on your LSAT.

Miscellaneous Games

Finally, seven LSAT tests between 1992 and 2003 included other miscellaneous games that do not neatly fall into one of the five primary game types. These include visualizing a map or variations on Matching or In-and-Out Games.

Variations on the Five Primary Game Types

Some games appear at first glance to not fit into one of the five standard game types. For example, consider a game in which eight people are to be seated around a table. This appears to be a "circle" game, but in fact you can set it up and solve it as though it were a standard linear Ordering Game. Simply draw the eight seats in a row and remember that the two "ends" of your linear diagram are seated next to each other.

Rather than making a new category of circle games for the two games that look like this, remain adaptive. Working with fewer (broad) categories of Logic Games will likely help you more than working with many (narrow) categories. You could likely define dozens of categories and subcategories to organize every LSAT Logic Game. However, while this might help you sort them in your notebook, it would be counterproductive to your goal of preparing for the unknown that awaits you on test day.

The best preparation for test day is to reinforce a big picture understanding of what Logic Games are testing, which is your ability to apply a set of rules to factual scenarios, using deductive reasoning to draw logical conclusions. Let the categories of Ordering, Stacked, Division, Matching, and In-and-Out guide your setup when you happen to see games that fall into these categories, but let common sense and your ability to work Logic Games prevail when you see something new.

Questions marked with a star are official LSAT questions provided by the LSAC.

Ordering Games

★ **14.** **C) is correct.** This is a general question. Look over the diagram, and then read through the answers to find one that violates the rules. We know for sure that the four variables H, N, K, and J must all come before G. The rules state that Nader and James joined before Gregg, that King joined before James, and that Hodges joined before Nader. Thus, there is no way Gregg could have joined in 1964 if he joined *after* Nader and James.

We know it is possible that Hodges could have joined in 1961 because the H variable could be placed in column 1. There is no sure indication that any other partners came before him, according to the diagram, so choice A) must be wrong. We also know choice B) is wrong: Hodges may also have joined in 1963— the H can be placed in column 3. This is because K could be in 1961 (column 1) and J could be in 1962 (column 2). We do not know for sure which of the partners joined first, but we do know that Hodges, King, and James all joined before Gregg and MacNeil. D) is also incorrect because MacNeil may have joined in 1964. The M variable can go in column 4; K, J, and H could come before it. Finally, choice E) is incorrect. O can go in 1964 because K, H, and N could come before it.

★ **15.** **E) is correct.** This is a hypothetical question. Draw a scenario in your diagram's workspace using the new information (J is in column 2, which stands for 1962). Look at your rules that relate to J and add in what you know (K must be in 1961 because King joined the firm before James). By doing that before you look at the answers, you save yourself from having to repeat the same thought process on every single answer choice. We cannot figure out anything else, so now look through the answers and find one that violates the rules. Hodges might have joined in 1963, so H can go in column 3. No variables must come before H, making A) incorrect. M can go in 1963; no variables must come before it, making B) incorrect. H can go in 1964, because M could come before it in 1963, making C) incorrect. N can go in 1964, because H could come before it in 1963, making D) incorrect. E) must be correct: O must be placed after both H and N, so the soonest it could be placed is in column 5, meaning the earliest Owens could have joined is 1965. It follows that it cannot be true that Owens joined in 1964.

> ### 💡 HELPFUL HINT
> Many people miss question 16 by forgetting about Owens. If you look to see who must come after James (as opposed to who could come before James), then you will not run the risk of making this mistake.

Exhibit 10.

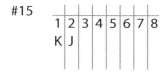

#15

1	2	3	4	5	6	7	8
K	J						

★ **16.** **D) is correct.** This is a general question. To determine the latest year that James could have joined and into which column J can go, look at the original rules to see how many partners joined *after* J. Then count backward from 1968 to arrive at the answer. Three variables must come after J: G, M, and I. So, the latest J could have joined is in 1965.

★ **17.** **B) is correct.** This is a hypothetical question. The question asks us to determine the number of partners for whom it is possible to figure out when they joined the firm. As in question 15, diagram a scenario using the new information (O is in 1965 and M is in 1967). Then, look at the remaining rules and add in what you know. It may help to redraw your remaining variables to make this clear:

Exhibit 11.

H – N
          ⟩ G – I
K – J

We do not know the order of H, K, N, and J, so there's no use trying to force those variables into positions. However, of the remaining variables, it is clear that I must be last, and G must be second to last. Therefore, I goes in 1968 and G goes in 1966. This question asks how many *other* variables we can place in our diagram (based on the new information they gave us), so the answer must be two.

★ **18.** **D) is correct.** This is an add-a-rule question. The easiest thing to do is to tack on the rule to your original diagram. Questions that change, add, or remove a rule will always be last, so you can change your original diagram without messing up future questions.

M is written twice here, which is generally something you want to avoid. However, in this case it would be a little tricky to add on the new rule without crossing lines over each other. The question is asking us the earliest possible position for M, so we do the opposite of what we did on question 16: we look to see how many other variables must come before M. In this case, H, N, O, K, and J must all come before M, so the earliest that MacNeil could have joined is 1966.

Exhibit 12.

                    O – M*
H – N ⟨ G – I
K – J ⟨ M*

Stacked Games

★ **19.** **E) is correct.** This is a hypothetical question. Draw a scenario in which you put R in line 3 for January. Recall the rule that one line 3 ticket must be G. Infer answer E: the line 3 tickets for February are G.

★ **20.** **A) is correct.** This is a hypothetical question. Draw a scenario in which you put G in line 2 for February (it cannot be January because line 2 for January is already P). We know that one line 3 ticket must be G, and it cannot be in February because then you would have two February tickets of the same color. Therefore, the line 3 tickets for January are G. One January ticket must be R, so answer A) must be true.

★ **21.** **A) is correct.** This is a general question. Answer A) can be true because January can use R, P, and Y, in that order. All four of the other answers are impossible. B) is wrong because February needs one each of G, R, and Y (it cannot use P). C) is wrong because this would prevent a red January ticket (this says *only* line 2 tickets are red, not line 2 tickets are red). D) is wrong because there would be no red January ticket. Finally, E) is wrong because February cannot have any P.

★ **22.** **B) is correct.** You could have Y/P/R for January and R/Y/G for February. Answer A) is wrong because one of the line 3 tickets must be green. Answers C) and D) are wrong because there would not be enough room to have both a red January ticket and a green line 3 ticket. Answer E) is wrong because there would not be enough room for a red January ticket.

★ **23.** **E) is correct.** This is a hypothetical question. Draw a scenario in which you put Y in line 3 for February. Infer G in line 3 for January. Infer R in line 1 for January. Infer R is not line 1 for February, so it must be line 2 for February. Therefore, G is line 1 for February.

Exhibit 13.

	1	2	3
J:	R	P	G
F:	G	R	Y

Based on this work, all of the answers must be true except for E), which must be false since we were able to fully determine every ticket set.

★ **24.** **C) is correct.** The green tickets could be in lines 1 and 3. This is a delete-a-rule question. Removing P leaves you with G, R, and Y for both months. Then we have a general question: what could be true? A) must be false because G, R, and Y must occur in each month (we only have three colors). B) must be false for the same reason as A). D) must be false because this would force two Ys to be in line 3. E) must be false because this would force two Rs to be in line 1.

Division Games

★ **1.** **D) is correct.** This is a general question, and it is traditionally the first question that appears on most logic games. Use your rules to eliminate answers. The first rule, "R must be added to class 1," does not eliminate any answers. The second rule, "S must be added to class 3," eliminates choice B). The third rule, "Neither S nor W can be added to the same class as Y," eliminates choice E). The fourth rule, "V cannot be added to the same class as Z," eliminates choice C). The last rule, "If T is added to class 1, Z must also be added to class 1," eliminates choice A). This leaves answer choice D), the correct choice.

★ 2. **E) is correct.** This is a general question. We do not know anything about V other than that it does not go with Z, and we do not know where Z goes. Do not make this question any harder than it is; without additional information, V could go in any of the three classes, so the correct answer is E).

★ 3. **A) is correct.** This is a hypothetical question. Draw a scenario in your diagram's workspace using the new information ("X is in class 1"). Then, look at your rules that pertain to X (there are none) or to class 1 ("If T, then Z"). Infer that T cannot be in class 1. Complete this thought: if T cannot be in class 1, where can it go? If T were in class 3, this would cause a problem (V and Z would have to split, with one filling up class 1 and the other going in class 2, but then W and Y would have to be together in class 2). Since T cannot be in class 3, it must be in class 2.

★ 4. **E) is correct.** This is a hypothetical question. If X goes in class 3, T *must* go in class 2. Otherwise, T and Z both would need to be in class 1. That would put W and Y together, which is not allowed.

 **DID YOU KNOW?**

When you are confronted with five answer choices that appear similar at first glance (as in question 6), take a step back and see what distinguishes them. On "five if" must be true questions, it is often the case that the right answer will involve placing unrestricted variables in positions where they cause a reaction among the remaining variables.

Exhibit 14.

	1	2	3
	(T → 2)		
	R _ _	_ _ _	S A̶
#4	R ½ W̶	½ W̶ T	S X
#5	R ½ W̶	½ W̶ X	S T
#6	R V X	_ _ _	S _

★ 5. **C) is correct.** This is a hypothetical question. If T goes in class 3, X must go in class 2. Create a scenario with T in class 3. As in question 4, V and Z must be kept separate, as must W and Y. Writing V/Z in a space in both class 1 and class 2 is a good way to diagram this; do the same with W/Y. The only variable remaining is X, and the only space remaining is in class 2. Thus, the answer is C).

★ 6. **D) is correct.** This is a general question. Some call this a "five if" question because all five answer choices are hypothetical (if) statements. As with any "must be true" question, you should not test the answers to see if they *could* be true. Instead, you can rule out an answer by showing that it could be false. For answer choice A), for example, plug in the "if" clause. What happens *if* T and X are added to class 2? Then, apply the rules. Is it possible to put V anywhere other than class 3? In this scenario, V can go in class 1 or class 2, so A) is not the answer. Repeat this process for the five answer choices until you find an answer where plugging in the "if" clause and applying the rules *forces* the "then" clause to follow. This is the case with answer choice D). Adding V and X to class 1 forces Y to go in class 2 because Y can never be with S. With Y in class 2, W *must* go in class 3.

Matching Games

★ 7. **E) is correct.** This is a general question, not the typical first question, but rather a "must be false" question based off of our diagram. Answers A) through D) are all *possible*; they all *could* be true. Answer E) absolutely must be false because N can only have one symptom (see previous step 6).

★ 8. **C) is correct.** This is a general question that asks for a pair of variables that can have the exact same number of and kinds of symptoms. For example, J and L would be a valid answer because they could both have headache, sneezing, and no fever. Of the answers provided, only C) is plausible. We already know that K and N must both have exactly one symptom (remember, if N had two or more, then it would be impossible for L to have two or more). It is certainly possible that K and N have the same symptom. Answer A) fails because J has two symptoms and N has one. Choice B) is incorrect because K has one symptom while L has two. Choice D) fails because L has two symptoms while M has three. Finally, choice E) is incorrect because M has three symptoms while N has one.

★ 9. **D) is correct.** This is a hypothetical question. First, plug in the new information, which is that L is not exactly the same (in number and types of symptoms) as anyone else. We already know that L does not have the same *number* of symptoms as K, M, or N. The only concern is that L cannot have the same *types* of symptoms as J, who (like L) has two symptoms. In order for L to avoid having both headache and sneezing like J does, L must have fever. Answer A) reflects this.

★ 10. **E) is correct.** This is a general question. Answer choice E) must be true because M has all three symptoms, and N has exactly one symptom. Many people mistakenly choose answer choice A), but J and L *could* have two symptoms in common. The question asks which pair shares exactly one symptom: two is not *exactly* one.

★ 11. **E) is correct.** This is a hypothetical question. First, examine the new information, which is that an individual has exactly two, but not all three, symptoms. What does this tell us? Well, we know that the person could not have illness M, because M requires all three symptoms. We also know that Walter could not have both J and K because that would require all three symptoms as well. Nor could Walter have both L and N, because L and N have no symptoms in common. Answer choice E) reflects the last inference: someone would have to have three symptoms in order to have both L and N.

In-and-Out Games

★ 1. **D) is correct.** This is a general question, and it is the traditional "first question" that appears on most logic games. Use your handwritten rules to eliminate the four wrong answers. The first rule ("H → ~L ~I ~K") eliminates answer choices A), B), and C). The next rule ("I → L M ~J ~H") eliminates answer choice E). That leaves choice D).

★ **2.**   **D) is correct.** This is a hypothetical question. First, apply your rules to the new information in the question:

Diagram for hypothetical questions 2, 4, 5, and 6 (new information in each question is <u>underlined</u>):

	In	Out
#2:	K <u>N</u> I L M	J H
#4:	H	<u>M</u> K I L
#5:	J N	K I L
#6:		<u>L</u> I K

The question tells us that K and N are in. Look at the rules for K and N: I, L, and M must also be in, while H must be out. Thus, the answer is choice D).

★ **3.**   **C) is correct.** This is a hypothetical question. The new information states that exactly three members are in. This means we cannot have a situation that would require more than three people. For example, K cannot be in. Choice C) accomplishes the same result: if I and N are in, then L and M would also have to be in, but that would be four people.

★ **4.**   **B) is correct.** This is a hypothetical question. First, apply your rules to the new information in the question (as in the diagram above). The question tells us that M is out. Apply your rule for ~M ("~M → H"). Since H is in, you then apply your rule for H and infer that K, I, and L are out. The answer must be choice B) because only H, J, and N could be in.

★ **5.**   **D) is correct.** This is a hypothetical question. If J and N are in, then K, I, and L must be out, so the answer is D). Questions like this take no time at all if you have taken your time to process the rules of the game.

★ **6.**   **E) is correct.** This is a hypothetical question. The new information is that L is out, but which rule do you look at? You do not have a rule for ~L, and the rule for "L is in" has no application when L is out. (Note: make sure to not commit a mistaken negation by assuming that if L is out, then J and H are in; this is a fallacy). The answer is that you should look at your rules to see which other variables *require* L. That is, where does L appear on the *right* side of an "if... then" arrow? Here, I and K require L. This is important because then we know that if L is out, I and K must also be out. The answer is thus E).

★ **7.**   **D) is correct.** This is a change-a-rule question. If the wording of the question was difficult for you, take time to break apart the clauses in the first sentence and understand what the question is asking of you. The question tells us that we are removing one condition and adding a new condition. Which condition are we removing? "~M → H." What are we adding? "Only if Nancy participates can Kevin fail to participate." This is the same as "Kevin is out only if Nancy is in" = ~K → N = ~N → K.

Here's the trick: when you remove "~M → H," you must also remove its contrapositive "~H → M" and the inferences that came from the rule (the M's required by I, K, and L). Then, add the new rule (including its contrapositive form) and make connections (adding an N everywhere you have a ~K).

As is often the case, the rule substitution here has no great effect on the outcome of the question: as before, there are four members who could participate with K—I, L, M, and N—so the answer is D).

5 Reading Comprehension: The Big Picture

There are two major components of a Reading Comprehension section: the **passages** and the **questions**. Four sets of questions must be completed, with five to eight questions per set, for a total of twenty-six to twenty-eight questions per section. You have thirty-five minutes to complete the section.

Reading Comprehension questions are very similar to Logical Reasoning questions. In general, students who master Logical Reasoning generally have few problems with the Reading Comprehension questions.

The primary difference between the Logical Reasoning and Reading Comprehension questions is that the latter passages are longer. Many students find it difficult to both read the lengthy passage and answer its seven questions in under nine minutes. Therefore, this chapter focuses primarily on efficient and effective reading strategies to help you beat the clock.

The Passage

Four sets of questions will appear in the Reading Comprehension section.

- Three sets of questions will each follow a single, long passage that usually ranges from fifty to seventy lines of text (350 – 500 words).

- One set of questions is a **comparative reading** exercise. This set of questions follows a set of *two* shorter passages (200 – 275 words each) on the same or similar topics.

Comparative reading passages can appear at any point during the Reading Comprehension section.

Always read Reading Comprehension passages as arguments, never as mere informational summaries or explanations. Additional tips on how to read the passages are provided next.

The Questions

Following each passage (or set of Comparative Reading passages), you will have five to eight questions. Questions generally ask the following:

- What is the author's main point/main idea/main conclusion?

- What is the author's primary purpose?

- What is the purpose of a given paragraph, sentence, line number, or word?

- What is the author (or another party) committed to believing, based on the passage?

- What attitude must the author (or another party) hold toward a given proposition?

- Which of the following is stated in the passage? (These are called **Detail** questions.)

- Which of the following is implied by the passage? (These are called **Inference** questions.)

- Which of the following, if true, would strengthen or weaken the argument?

★ LSAT EXAM QUESTIONS

PrepTest 8, Questions 7 – 13

Gray marketing, the selling of trademarked products through channels of distribution not authorized by the trademark holder, can involve distribution of goods either within a market region or across market boundaries. Gray marketing within a market region ("channel flow diversion") occurs when manufacturer-authorized distributors sell trademarked goods to unauthorized distributors who then sell the goods to consumers within the same region. For example, quantity discounts from manufacturers may motivate authorized dealers to enter the gray market because they can purchase larger quantities of a product than they themselves intend to stock if they can sell the extra units through gray market channels.

When gray marketing occurs across market boundaries, it is typically in an international setting and may be called "parallel importing." Manufacturers often produce and sell products in more than one country and establish a network of authorized dealers in each country. Parallel importing occurs when trademarked goods intended for one country are diverted from proper channels (channel flow diversion) and then exported to unauthorized distributors in another country.

Trademark owners justifiably argue against gray marketing practices since such practices clearly jeopardize the goodwill established by trademark owners: consumers who purchase trademarked goods in the gray market do not get the same "extended product," which typically includes pre- and post-sale service. Equally important, authorized distributors may cease to promote the product if it becomes available for much lower prices through unauthorized channels.

Current debate over regulation of gray marketing focuses on three disparate theories in trademark law that have been variously and confusingly applied to parallel importation cases: universality, exhaustion, and territoriality. The theory of universality holds that a trademark is only an indication of the source or origin of the product. This theory does not recognize the goodwill functions of a trademark. When the courts apply this theory, gray marketing practices are allowed to continue because the origin of the product remains the same regardless of the specific route of the product through the channel of distribution. The exhaustion theory holds that a trademark owner relinquishes all rights once a product has been sold. When this theory is applied, gray marketing practices are allowed to continue because the trademark owners' rights cease as soon as their products are sold to a distributor. The theory of territoriality holds that a trademark is effective in the country in which it is registered. Under the theory of territoriality, trademark owners can stop gray marketing practices in the registering countries on products bearing their trademarks. Since only the territoriality theory affords trademark owners any real legal protection against gray marketing practices, I believe it is inevitable as well as desirable that it will come to be consistently applied in gray marketing cases.

7. Which one of the following best expresses the main point of the passage?

    A) Gray marketing is unfair to trademark owners and should be legally controlled.

    B) Gray marketing is practiced in many different forms and places, and legislators should recognize the futility of trying to regulate it.

    C) The mechanisms used to control gray marketing across markets are different from those most effective in controlling gray marketing within markets.

    D) The three trademark law theories that have been applied in gray marketing cases lead to different case outcomes.

    E) Current theories used to interpret trademark laws have resulted in increased gray marketing activity.

8. The function of the passage as a whole is to

    A) criticize the motives and methods of those who practice gray marketing.

    B) evaluate the effects of both channel flow diversion and parallel importation.

    C) discuss the methods that have been used to regulate gray marketing and evaluate such methods' degrees of success.

    D) describe a controversial marketing practice and evaluate several legal views regarding it.

    E) discuss situations in which certain marketing practices are common and analyze the economic factors responsible for their development.

9. Which one of the following does the author offer as an argument against gray marketing?

    A) Manufacturers find it difficult to monitor the effectiveness of promotional efforts made on behalf of products that are gray marketed.

    B) Gray marketing can discourage product promotion by authorized dealers.

C) Gray marketing forces manufacturers to accept the low profit margins that result from quantity discounting.

D) Gray marketing discourages competition among unauthorized dealers.

E) Quality standards in the manufacture of products likely to be gray marketed may decline.

10. The information in the passage suggests that proponents of the theory of territoriality would probably differ from proponents of the theory of exhaustion on which one of the following issues?

A) The right of trademark owners to enforce, in countries in which the trademarks are registered, distribution agreements intended to restrict distribution to authorized channels.

B) The right of trademark owners to sell trademarked goods only to those distributors who agree to abide by distribution agreements.

C) The legality of channel flow diversion that occurs in a country other than the one in which a trademark is registered.

D) The significance consumers attach to a trademark.

E) The usefulness of trademarks as marketing tools.

11. The author discusses the impact of gray marketing on goodwill in order to

A) fault trademark owners for their unwillingness to offer a solution to a major consumer complaint against gray marketing.

B) indicate a way in which manufacturers sustain damage against which they ought to be protected.

C) highlight one way in which gray marketing across markets is more problematic than gray marketing within a market.

D) demonstrate that gray marketing does not always benefit the interests of unauthorized distributors.

E) argue that consumers are unwilling to accept a reduction in price in exchange for elimination of service.

12. The author's attitude toward the possibility that the courts will come to exercise consistent control over gray marketing practices can best be characterized as one of

A) resigned tolerance.

B) utter dismay.

C) reasoned optimism.

D) unbridled fervor.

E) cynical indifference.

13. It can be inferred from the passage that some channel flow diversion might be eliminated if

A) profit margins on authorized distribution of goods were less than those on goods marketed through parallel importing.

B) manufacturers relieved authorized channels of all responsibility for product promotion.

C) manufacturers charged all authorized distributors the same unit price for products regardless of quantity purchased.

D) the post-sale service policies of authorized channels were controlled by manufacturers.

E) manufacturers refused to provide the "extended product" to consumers who purchase goods in the gray market.

★ LSAT EXAM QUESTIONS

PrepTest 55, Questions 7 – 13

The following passages concern a plant called purple loosestrife. Passage A is excerpted from a report issued by a prairie research council; passage B is from a journal of sociology.

Passage A

Purple loosestrife (*Lythrum salicaria*), an aggressive and invasive perennial of Eurasian origin, arrived with settlers in eastern North America in the early 1800s and has spread across the continent's midlatitude wetlands. The impact of purple loosestrife on native vegetation has been disastrous, with more than 50 percent of the biomass of some wetland communities displaced. Monospecific blocks of this weed have maintained themselves for at least twenty years. Impacts on wildlife have not been well studied, but serious reductions in waterfowl and aquatic furbearer productivity have been observed. In addition, several endangered species of vertebrates are threatened with further degradation of their breeding habitats. Although purple loosestrife can invade relatively undisturbed habitats, the spread and dominance of this weed have been greatly accelerated in disturbed habitats. While digging out the plants can temporarily halt their spread, there has been little research on long-term purple loosestrife control. Glyphosate has been used successfully, but no measure of the impact of this herbicide on native plant communities has been made.

With the spread of purple loosestrife growing exponentially, some form of integrated control is needed. At present, coping with purple loosestrife hinges on early detection of the weed's arrival in areas, which allows local eradication to be carried out with minimum damage to the native plant community.

Passage B

The war on purple loosestrife is apparently conducted on behalf of nature, an attempt to liberate the biotic community from the tyrannical influence of a life-destroying invasive weed. Indeed, purple loosestrife control is portrayed by its practitioners as an environmental initiative intended to save nature rather than control it. Accordingly, the purple loosestrife literature, scientific and otherwise, dutifully discusses the impacts of the weed on endangered species—and on threatened biodiversity more generally. Purple loosestrife is a pollution, according to the scientific community, and all of nature suffers under its pervasive influence.

Regardless of the perceived and actual ecological effects of the purple invader, it is apparent that popular pollution ideologies have been extended into the wetlands of North America. Consequently, the scientific effort to liberate nature from purple loosestrife has failed to decouple itself from its philosophical origin as an instrument to control nature to the satisfaction of human desires. Birds, particularly game birds and waterfowl, provide the bulk of the justification for loosestrife management. However, no bird species other than the canvasback has been identified in the literature as endangered by purple loosestrife. The impact of purple loosestrife on furbearing mammals is discussed at great length, though none of the species highlighted (muskrat, mink) can be considered threatened in North America. What is threatened by purple loosestrife is the economics of exploiting such preferred species and the millions of dollars that will be lost to the economies of the United States and Canada from reduced hunting, trapping, and recreation revenues due to a decline in the production of the wetland resource.

7. Both passages explicitly mention which one of the following?

   A) furbearing animals

   B) glyphosate

   C) the threat purple loosestrife poses to economies

   D) popular pollution ideologies

   E) literature on purple loosestrife

8. Each of the passages contains information sufficient to answer which one of the following questions?

   A) Approximately how long ago did purple loosestrife arrive in North America?

   B) Is there much literature discussing the potential benefit that hunters might derive from purple loosestrife management?

   C) What is an issue regarding purple loosestrife management on which both hunters and farmers agree?

   D) Is the canvasback threatened with extinction due to the spread of purple loosestrife?

   E) What is a type of terrain that is affected in at least some parts of North America by the presence of purple loosestrife?

9. It can be inferred that the authors would be most likely to disagree about which one of the following?

   A) Purple loosestrife spreads more quickly in disturbed habitats than in undisturbed habitats.

   B) The threat posed by purple loosestrife to local aquatic furbearer populations is serious.

   C) Most people who advocate that eradication measures be taken to control purple loosestrife are not genuine in their concern for the environment.

   D) The size of the biomass that has been displaced by the purple loosestrife is larger than is generally thought.

   E) Measures should be taken to prevent other nonnative plant species from invading North America.

10. Which one of the following most accurately describes the attitude expressed by the author of passage B toward the overall argument represented by passage A?

    A) enthusiastic agreement

    B) cautious agreement

    C) pure neutrality

    D) general ambivalence

    E) pointed skepticism

11. It can be inferred that both authors would be most likely to agree with which one of the following statements regarding purple loosestrife?

   A) As it increases in North America, some wildlife populations tend to decrease.

   B) Its establishment in North America has had a disastrous effect on native North America.

   C) It is very difficult to control effectively with herbicides.

   D) Its introduction into North America was a great ecological blunder.

   E) When it is eliminated from a given area, it tends to return to that area fairly quickly.

12. Which one of the following is true about the relationship between the two passages?

   A) Passage A presents evidence that directly counters claims made in passage B.

   B) Passage B assumes what passage A explicitly argues for.

   C) Passage B displays an awareness of the arguments touched on in passage A, but not vice versa.

   D) Passage B advocates a policy that passage A rejects.

   E) Passage A downplays the seriousness of claims made in passage B.

13. Which one of the following, if true, would cast doubt on the argument in passage B, but bolster the argument in passage A?

   A) Localized population reduction is often a precursor to widespread endangerment of a species.

   B) Purple loosestrife was barely noticed in North America before the advent of suburban sprawl in the 1950s.

   C) The amount by which overall hunting, trapping, and recreation revenues would be reduced as a result of the extinction of one or more species threatened by purple loosestrife represents a significant portion of those revenues.

   D) Some environmentalists who advocate taking measures to eradicate purple loosestrife view such measures as a means of controlling nature.

   E) Purple loosestrife has never become a problem in its native habitat, even though no effort has been made to eradicate it there.

Five Tips for Effective Reading

Reading Comprehension passages generally fall into one of four broad categories:

- humanities
- social sciences
- life sciences
- issues related to the law

You are not expected to have any background knowledge of the passage content. In fact, background knowledge can be a hindrance when you subconsciously read additional outside information into the passage. Be careful to focus only on what the passage actually says.

A common misconception is that the Reading Comprehension passages are descriptive, informational articles, when every Reading Comprehension passage is actually persuasive. This means that you will need to distinguish an author's premises from the conclusions.

As you read, do the following:

1. Keep your pencil in hand. When you read something that sounds like a conclusion, put it in brackets. When you see extreme language, circle it. When you notice two facts that work together to make an interesting inference, write it down. Get things out of your head and on paper. See "Recommended Symbols for Annotation" in Table 5.1.

2. Read the passage for structure, not to memorize the details. Focus on the logical components of the passage: for instance, where is the author's main conclusion (if there is one)? Where are the intermediate conclusions? Who are the different parties with their perspectives? That way, if you need specific details to answer a question, you can quickly spot that information in the passage.

3. At the end of the first paragraph, stop and make sure you thoroughly understand what the author has said. The first paragraph generally presents one of three things:
    o   The author's conclusion, which will then be supported in the following paragraphs.
    o   Another person's point of view, which the author will then accept or refute in the following paragraphs.
    o   A problem or situation, which the author will attempt to solve or explain in the following paragraphs.

    Understanding the first paragraph is crucial to understanding the function of the passage as a whole. If you are confused by the first paragraph, read it again for understanding.

4. After you finish reading each paragraph, take three to five seconds to write a few words about the paragraph. If the author was comparing Tuscan art to Venetian art and decided that Tuscan art was more widely renowned in the eighteenth century, you might write "T > V" in the margin to summarize the author's thoughts. Short margin annotations can be instrumental in marking details you may need to find later. Annotations also help your brain analyze the big picture of the argument.

5. At the end of the whole passage, stop and spend ten to twenty seconds thinking about the answers to these two questions:
    o   What is the author's main point?
    o   What is the author's primary purpose?

    These questions are discussed in detail later in the chapter. Knowing them can save you several minutes in answering the passage's multiple-choice questions.

TABLE 5.1. Recommended Symbols for Annotation in the Margin

SYMBOL	MEANING	USAGE
→	if...then	Diagram conditional statements. Just as in Logical Reasoning and Logic Games, you will be expected to make inferences, and conditional statements often lead to such inferences.
+ –	positive attitude negative attitude	Notice where the author makes his or her personal feelings known about a subject by using words with positive or negative connotations, such as: "This **inspirational** work..." or "Smith's study portrays an **alarming** phenomenon..."
V$_{Auth}$ V$_B$ V$_C$	Viewpoint	Keep the various viewpoints in the passage distinct. Some questions ask you for the view of someone other than the author.
ex.	Example	Section off lengthy examples from the rest of the passage. Use an arrow pointing from the example to the sentence in the passage that the example is supporting. Remember: Examples are premises.
[ ]	Conclusion	Put brackets around all conclusions, whether the author's or another's.
⬭	transitions premise/conclusion indicators	Circle transition words such as: **But, However, Nevertheless, Yet, On the other hand**, etc., as well as premise and conclusion indicators.

Question Types

Main Point

Often, the first question in the set of questions that follows the passage will ask you something like:

> Which of the following best expresses the main idea of the passage?

When you stop to consider the main idea, put yourself in the author's shoes. If you were the author, and if you had to replace the entire passage with one sentence that would prove your point, what would you say? Focus primarily on the author's conclusion, as opposed to the premises. What is the author trying to prove?

 DID YOU KNOW?

The main point and the author's primary purpose are distinct. The **main point** is the main idea of a passage—the author's thesis, his or her main conclusion. On the other hand, the **author's primary purpose** is the function of the passage, or what the author intends the passage to accomplish.

As discussed earlier, you should always stop to consider the author's main point after reading the passage, even if you're short on time, or there is not an explicit "main point" question. Identify the author's argument so you can better answer the questions about what the author believes.

Primary Purpose

Following many passages, one of the questions will ask you something like:

> Which of the following describes the primary purpose of the passage? Which of the following most accurately characterizes the function of the passage?

When you stop to consider the primary purpose of the passage, put yourself in the position of a critic. Pretend someone has just asked you to describe why the author has written the passage. You should respond with a simple verb phrase, like

- to present new evidence.
- to question a common assumption.
- to refute a hypothesis.
- to critique a recently released book.
- to showcase the various viewpoints in a scholarly debate.
- to evaluate a theory and the charges of its critics.

Use Method of Reasoning language to describe the function of the passage. Whereas Main Point answers tend to be lengthy (like thesis sentences), Primary Purpose answers can be as short as four words.

Purpose of a Paragraph, Lines, or Words

These questions are similar to Primary Purpose questions, except that they focus on a specific paragraph, certain lines, or certain words in the passage. Answer questions about a specific paragraph just like you would answer a question about the primary passage as a whole: by considering, in one verb phrase (with an infinitive verb and a direct object), *why* the author is writing that paragraph. Do this *before* you look at the answer choices so that they do not distract you.

Be careful with questions that ask about specific line numbers, as in the following example:

> The author most likely refers to birds (lines 31 – 33) in order to do what?

First, go back to the passage to find the reference that the question mentions. But do not simply read the lines mentioned. Read one sentence before and one sentence after. Realize that the question is not asking you to define what the author is saying in lines 31 – 33. Rather, the question is asking you why the author has included the sentence in lines 31 – 33. Usually, the answer is something like:

- "It is an example of [the point the author is trying to make in lines 29 – 30]," or
- "It is offered in support of [the point the author is trying to make in lines 34 – 35]."

Very often, one of the wrong answers will look like an interpretation of whatever the author has actually said in lines 31 – 33. *Beware*: Explaining the meaning of the author's sentence does not answer the question of the purpose of the author's sentence. Always read up one and down one additional sentence, and look for the logical connection between the line numbers in question and the remainder of the passage.

Many questions ask you about a specific word, for example:

- The use of the word *deviation* (line 24) serves primarily to:
- The author uses the word *transitory* (line 8) most closely to mean:

First, go back to the passage and see how the word is used in context. In these two sample questions, the first asks for the word's *purpose* (so look before and after the word for clues as to its logical function), while the second asks for the word's *definition*.

Author's Belief

Consider this question:

> It can be inferred from the passage that the author most likely believes which of the following?

Here, the key is to treat this question as a simple "What must be true?" question. Very frequently, students pick an answer consistent with the passage, but not an answer that follows from the passage.

If you treat these questions like Must Be True questions, you will find it easier to eliminate four answers and choose the remaining answer; otherwise, you might find that two or three of the answer choices look equally plausible.

Author's Attitude

Consider this question:

> The author most probably holds which of the following attitudes toward spelunking?

Generally, these questions have five answer choices that span a spectrum, like

A) wild enthusiasm

B) overt optimism

C) qualified approval

D) reluctant disapproval

E) intransigent scorn

In most cases, extreme answers like A) and E) are not correct. However, if a word or phrase in the passage indicates that one of these is the answer, then pick the extreme answer. This is where using the + and – in the margins to annotate attitude-indicator words comes in handy.

Questions about the author's attitude or what the author would agree with are not subjective. You should read these questions as saying, "Based on the passage, what does the author absolutely have to believe?" or "What attitude must the author hold because of what the author has written?"

Many students have trouble with Reading Comprehension because they feel that they are supposed to be able to read the author's mind. In reality, you only need to read the text and make the logical inferences that reasonably follow from what has been explicitly stated.

Detail Questions

Consider this question:

> All of the following are specifically mentioned in the passage
> EXCEPT:

This traditional Reading Comprehension exercise tests your ability to remember where to find specific details in the passage. Frequently, these are EXCEPT questions, requiring you to find four of the five answer choices in the passage, before choosing the remaining answer choice.

Inference Questions

Consider this question:

> It can be inferred from the passage that:

These are the Reading Comprehension equivalent of Must Be True questions. Treat them accordingly, basing your answer entirely and only on facts stated in the passage. Watch out for extreme language in the answer choices, and pick an answer that is worded modestly.

Strengthen and Weaken Questions

Consider these questions:

> Which of the following, if true, would lend the most support to the
> author's hypothesis? Which of the following, if true, would most
> seriously undermine the validity of the author's research?

Just as in Logical Reasoning Strengthen and Weaken questions, you will be asked to bring in outside information to bolster or attack the author's argument. Remember that every LSAT Reading Comprehension passage is an argument. Also, remember to never cross out an answer choice because it "isn't true"; the questions here tell you to assume that the answers are true.

Other Questions

Although not as common, other questions will ask you to describe the organization of the passage or a specific paragraph. These questions are similar to Role of a Statement or Method of Reasoning questions, but you must choose an answer that lists the correct sequence of components that appear in the passage.

Additionally, some questions ask you to complete an analogy by identifying which of the five answer choices is most analogous to a situation in the passage. These questions are similar to Parallel Principle questions.

Recognize that you may see new and different questions on test day. Still, the vast majority of questions will be the types described above. Because there are five to eight questions (of a generally predictable nature) following each passage, it is not worth your time to read all the questions before you read the passage. Just read the passage, annotate as you go, and follow the tips presented earlier to ensure that you are looking for relevant information as you read.

Comparative Reading: Passages and Questions

Sometimes, the two passages come from authors who are writing on the same issue. In such a case, they may either be writing opposing arguments, or they may be arguing the same conclusion but for different reasons. Alternatively, you might have two authors whose passages are related because they cover a common subject, but they do not actually argue the same specific issue; for example, one might be writing about teaching law, while the other might be writing about teaching history. Identify the authors' relationship to each other *as you read* because you will likely be asked about how one of the authors views the other, or about the relationship of one passage to the other.

Time Management

There are generally two strategies for time management on Reading Comprehension:

1. Attempt to read all four passages and answer all the questions.

    This is the path you should take if you have little or no trouble reading the passages and answering the questions within thirty-five minutes. Plan to spend eight minutes and forty-five seconds on each of the four passages—a little less if the passage only has five or six questions, and a little longer if the passage has eight questions. Generally, it is a good idea to spend three minutes to three minutes and forty-five seconds reading the passage, then ten to twenty seconds considering the main point and primary purpose, using the remaining four minutes and thirty seconds to five minutes and thirty seconds to answer the questions.

2. Choose the three passages you prefer, and aim for near–100 percent accuracy on their questions.

    If you find reading through the passage in four minutes or less difficult, then you might aim to answer only three of the four sets of questions (all of them correctly). If you do this, you should try to reduce the number of questions you would miss by skipping either the passage that has the fewest questions or the passage that looks the most difficult. You may find that completing three passages well can earn you more points than you would be able to earn by attempting all four passages poorly.

Finally, as in Logical Reasoning, work efficiently on the questions. When you are asked about a specific fact from the passage, an inference about a topic that was discussed, or a specific paragraph or line number, go to the passage, consider the question, and anticipate the answer.

Do this before you start sifting through answer choices! You will have a better grasp of what the answer should look like, greater confidence in choosing an answer, and less difficulty in choosing between two answers that both look right.

Learning to Read Difficult Material

If you are not accustomed to reading difficult articles, and find yourself unable to digest the content of LSAT Reading Comprehension passages, then spend several weeks (ideally, three to four months) reading dense, scholarly material. For example, you might consider reading the online version of the *Harvard Law Review*. Read quickly, paraphrase as you read, and practice typing out 350- to 500-word articles (in the style of LSAT Reading Comprehension passages) on the material that you read. Additionally, consider using the Reading Comprehension Worksheet on non-LSAT reading materials to practice your ability to identify arguments in day-to-day readings.

It is extremely important for you to understand the material you are reading. You cannot simply let your eyes pass over the page. Engage with the passages. Pretend you are arguing against the author. Become personally involved, and wrap your mind around the passage. If you fail to understand a sentence, you may very well lose the meaning of a paragraph, and you cannot afford to do this. Be diligent, keep your focus, and keep your pencil on the page.

Explanations for the correct answers are provided next. For the more difficult questions, explanations for the incorrect answers are also provided.

Questions marked with a star are official LSAT questions provided by the LSAC.

PrepTest 8, Questions 7 – 13 (Standard Reading Comprehension)

★ 7.   **A) is correct.** This is a Main Point question. The author is trying to prove that gray marketing harms trademark owners (third paragraph) and should be controlled (end of last paragraph, see "territoriality"). None of the remaining answers are supported by the passage.

★ 8.   **D) is correct.** This is a Primary Purpose question. The author first describes what gray marketing is, and then evaluates three legal views of how to regulate it. Answer A) is wrong because the author does not attack gray marketers' motives. Answer B) is wrong because the author does not weigh the merits of the effects of gray marketing. Answer C) is wrong because the author discusses legal theories, not methods of curtailing gray marketing. Answer E) is wrong because the second half (economic factors) of the answer is not present.

★ 9.   **B) is correct.** None of the remaining answers are details from the passage. This is a Detail question.

★ 10.   **A) is correct.** Proponents of territoriality believe that trademark owners can enforce their rights with the country of registration even after a product is sold. Proponents of exhaustion do not believe those rights exist after a product is sold. Protecting a distribution agreement against gray marketing would logically require the trademark owner to be able to enforce the trademark, even after the owner has sold the product to the initial authorized dealer, who then sells the product to the unauthorized dealer. This is an Inference question. The two groups might agree that B) is true (nobody is attempting to *restrict* owners' rights to sell goods). They might also agree that C) is true (there is no protection in another country). Answers D) and E) are irrelevant because they are not issues discussed in the passage.

★ 11.   **B) is correct.** This question asks why the author includes the discussion in the third paragraph about the impact of gray marketing. The correct answer is B) because the author is proving that trademark owners "justifiably" seek to stop gray marketing. The author is trying to prove that gray marketing harms manufacturers and should be stopped. This is a Purpose of Paragraph question.

★ 12.   **C) is correct.** This is an Attitude question. This question asks the author's attitude toward the likelihood of judicial control of gray marketing, which, based on the passage, the author finds likely. The answer is C) because the author is favorable. Answers A), B), and E) are incorrect because they are negative. Answer D) is too extreme; nothing in the passage sufficiently indicates unbridled fervor.

★ 13. **C) is correct.** This is an Inference question. Evidently, offering quantity discounts leads authorized dealers to purchase extra goods that they must then sell to unauthorized dealers, resulting in gray marketing. Logically, we can infer that if all goods cost the same, this incentive to engage in channel flow diversion would go away. Is it certain? No, but in this case, channel flow diversion *might* be eliminated, and that's what the question is asking.

PrepTest 55, Questions 7 – 13 (Comparative Reading Comprehension)

★ 7. **A) is correct.** Furbearing animals are mentioned in specific lines in the passage. This is a Detail question.

★ 8. **E) is correct.** According to the passage, purple loosestrife affects wetlands in at least some parts of North America. This is a Detail question.

★ 9. **B) is correct.** This is a Point at Issue question to which passage A's author would have to say, "Yes, that's true," while passage B's author would have to say, "No that's false."

★ 10. **E) is correct.** The author of passage B has a negative attitude toward the arguments of scientists who seek to "liberate nature from purple loosestrife." This is an Attitude question. Answers A) and B) are incorrect because they are positive answer choices. Answers C) and D) are neutral answer choices and therefore incorrect.

★ 11. **A) is correct.** Both authors must agree that some wildlife populations will decrease as purple loosestrife becomes more prevalent. The author of passage B concedes that some bird populations decrease but focuses on making the point that these birds (apart from the canvasback) are not endangered. The remaining answers are incorrect because the author of passage B would have no reason for commitment to any of them. This is an Inference question.

★ 12. **C) is correct.** The author of passage B responds directly to scientists who make the sort of argument that the author of passage A makes. The author of passage A, however, does not counter any of passage B's points, which they would do if they were aware of passage B's argument. This is a Relationship of the Passages question.

★ 13. **A) is correct.** If it were true that localized population reduction usually comes before widespread endangerment, passage B would be weakened because its argument depends upon the idea that purple loosestrife is primarily harming species that are not in real danger of extinction. At the same time, passage A would be strengthened by the extra support for controlling purple loosestrife early. This is a Weaken/Strengthen question.

6 | LSAT Writing Sample

What Is the LSAT Writing Sample?

The sixth and final section of the LSAT is always a thirty-five-minute essay, which the LSAT calls the Writing Sample. The Writing Sample is a straight-forward essay, in which you are called on to help someone choose between two options. The decision-maker has two goals that should guide your recommendation. The writing prompt includes these two goals as well as a paragraph of facts about each of the two options. Based only on the goals and facts stated in the prompt, you should construct a three- to five-paragraph essay in the space provided.

Is the Writing Sample Scored?

No. The Writing Sample does not count toward your LSAT score. However, this does not mean that you should dismiss the Writing Sample altogether. A copy of your Writing Sample from every LSAT you take will be forwarded to every law school to which you apply, so you should not leave the Writing Sample blank, write in a foreign language, respond to a different topic, or do anything else that would indicate your disregard for the written portion of the test.

Why Complete an Unscored Writing Sample?

Many students perform very well on the LSAT but cannot compose a proper paragraph or write a simple argument in which they state applicable rules, discuss the relevant facts, and then draw conclusions. This act of applying rules to facts in order to draw conclusions is the absolute essence of law school and lawyering, and law schools want to be sure that you have at least a fundamental understanding of what that entails.

While an excellent Writing Sample will not help a student overcome a poor LSAT score, it could make the difference between an admission and a waitlist (or denial) when you are up against several other candidates who appear otherwise similar on paper.

Tips for the Writing Sample

- Write your answer as though your reader is not intimately familiar with the goals and facts stated in the prompt. That is, do not be afraid to restate the goals and facts verbatim.

- Do not use quotation marks or citations when citing facts from the prompt.

- Avoid first-person narrative (which often sounds unprofessional).

Recommended Structure

- Start with a one- to three-sentence introductory paragraph in which you describe the decision to be made, the relevant goals, and your recommendation.

- In the next paragraph, discuss your (factual) reasons for the option you recommend, and refute the strongest counterarguments against your option.

- In the third paragraph, (factually) refute the strongest argument for the option you did not choose.

- End with a one-sentence conclusion, restating your recommendation and its factual basis.

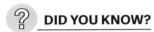

DID YOU KNOW?

Very minor errors in grammar and spelling are acceptable as long as the overall response is clearly structured and appropriately addresses the prompt.

Made in the USA
Las Vegas, NV
20 May 2022

49171672R00107